Foreword

The Rt Hon. the Lord Robertson of Port Ellen KT GCMG Hon FRSE PC (Secretary of State for Defence 1997–99, Secretary General of NATO 1999–2003)

We all know the great war stories – the deeds of inspirational bravery which make movies to be seen over and over again. We recognise and revere the great war leaders and personalities. Their names are in lights, on books and on statues. We have whole libraries devoted to the origins of wars and the impact the conflicts have had on our history.

But wars affect ordinary people in extraordinary ways as well. Lives are disrupted, affected and even ended by forces far from the lives of the man or woman in the street. People are taken from their peaceful way of life and faced with challenges they could never imagine. Some of the greatest stories – about the ability of accidental heroes to rise to dizzy heights of achievement – are never heard.

Here is one such story: three telephone engineers are plucked from obscurity and thrown into a maelstrom of adventure. The story has all the ingredients of a modern airport novel – courage, daring, sex, love, cunning, innocence, humour and incredible luck. But this is not fiction – it is for real. The three Scottish heroes of the action then returned to obscurity after their amazing exploits. For decades, because of the Official Secrets Act, the story could not be told. Luckily, sixty years later, one of them has published this account.

When I read this book in manuscript, I could not stop turning the pages. The early events made the old Scottish word 'gallus' come to mind, but as events unfold, you realise how determination, resourcefulness and sheer bravado can move mountains – or at least the bars of a prisoner of war camp.

Those of us who, almost every Christmas, watch The Great Escape would never have guessed that nearby three Scottish guys had been doing the same thing on the same day. And unlike the more famous escapees from Stalag Luft Drei, these three made it home.

At this point in history, anniversaries of the First and Second World Wars have brought home to a new generation how much we owe to those who gave up their comfortable lives so that we might live in peace and safety. Old men, and women too, with blazers and medals nowadays leaning on sticks are living legends. Ordinary people, like John McCallum, Jimmy O'Neill and Joe Harkin were called upon to do extraordinary things. And, collectively, they guaranteed our precious freedom.

This is a great tale – with a deep message. Read, enjoy – and reflect.

George Robertson

Preface

You've seen it on TV a dozen times, you may have read the book and, if you're old enough, you may have discussed it after it happened. When they filmed it, they called it *The Great Escape*.

What I cannot understand is who christened it with a name that is totally misleading. Rembrandt's painting 'The Man in the Golden Helmet' is a great masterpiece, as is Tolstoy's *War and Peace* a great piece of classical writing. The list of Greats that spring to mind is unending, but most of them were successful achievements.

There are exceptions to everything in life, like the Great Plague and the Great War, neither of which could have been great to anyone who was involved in them.

The dictionary quotes 'great' as meaning 'large, big, important or distinguished'. The Stalag Luft Drei escape was definitely big, but was only distinguished by the deaths of the fifty brave airmen who misguidedly made the attempt.

Truth being stranger than fiction, three Scots escaped from their camp at the same time as the sixty-seven airmen and, as luck would have it, they unfortunately chose a route which passed through the town of Sagan, which was the railhead for Stalag Three.

Just as the mass escape story is true, so also is the story of the three Glasgow men who escaped at the same time – they were my brother Jimmy, my friend Joe and myself.

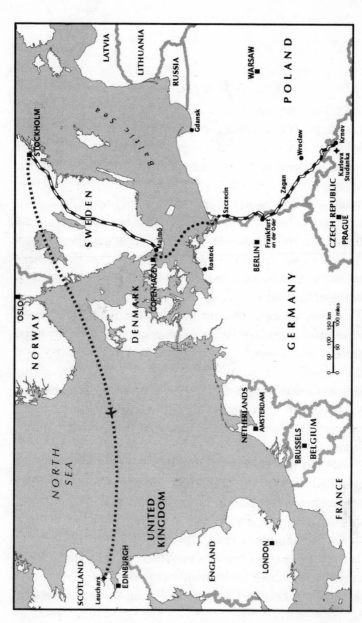

Map drawn by Mary Spence

1

When I reached the glorious age of nineteen, I signed up as a Supplementary Reservist with the Royal Corps of Signals, whose Drill Hall was situated in Yorkhill in Glasgow. I was merely following a family tradition, as my two older brothers had set the pattern for me previously. My brother, William, had completed his service but my brother, James O'Neill, was still in. The three of us were telephone engineers in the Post Office, so it made good sense to give our services to the Signal Corps and this particular unit consisted almost entirely of Post Office personnel.

This was when I first met Joe Harkin, who was already a Reservist, and from this time on, as long as we were in uniform, we were almost inseparable – Jimmy, Joe and Johnny.

Joe was a slim good-looking young man with wavy brown hair, fairly energetic and a few years older than myself. At that time he was an external lineman and, as I had joined the Corps in this capacity, we had something in common, including a mutual liking.

Brother Jimmy was a different type of character from Joe – slightly older, reddish blonde hair, mainly cool good-humoured nature, but with a temper which could flare and then disappear as quickly as it had come. He was the most solidly built of the three of us and, being the eldest, naturally assumed the lead figure in our trio.

I was the lightweight of the party in all departments – age, height and weight, with no distinguishing features that anyone would ever remember me by – which, in life, could also be an asset.

We were paid an annual bounty, which we received quarterly, and although it was not a lot, it did provide a new suit and a pair of shoes every year as long as you restricted yourself to the less expensive tailors. The money was laughingly referred to as 'Blood Money'. Much as I enjoyed spending this extra cash, little did I dream that the day of reckoning would come and that I would be called upon literally to repay in blood, with bullet-wound scars as a receipt for having paid up! But that, as they say, is another story.

It is strange to think that our lives are made up of stories of adventure, drama, romance and other things, and all these happenings are either gilded or eroded, sometimes enhanced, by our memory and imagination.

Jimmy, for instance, had spent some years in the Merchant Navy and so had a background of world travel, which stood us in very good stead later, as without his intimate knowledge of port operations and seamen's habits, we could not possibly have succeeded in our big adventure. After his time at sea, Jimmy took a job ashore and became a cable jointer with the Post Office, and this was the only difference between the three of us – Joe and I were external linemen and Jimmy was a cable specialist.

Being a lineman was, on the whole, very hard work. Imagine sitting at the top of a telephone pole in winter with a heavy safety belt supporting you and the steps cutting off the circulation to your feet, the wind and rain slowly freezing you, making for awkward cold hands. Yet I loved it: when my external training was completed, I was transferred to an internal section fitting switchboards. I wriggled, pleaded, cajoled and left no stone unturned to get back to the outdoor work that I so much enjoyed, but all to no avail. The rest of my time in the Engineering Department was spent doing work from which I derived no pleasure whatsoever.

However, the Royal Signals were willing to let me exercise my prowess at being a lineman. If I had thought that I had seen some hard times doing the job in a Scottish winter, what was still to come was devastating.

By the way, I suppose I should mention as background that Jimmy and Joe were both happily married and that I was a very inexperienced bachelor.

2

In September 1938 our unit was taking part in the Regular Army manoeuvres which were taking place in Southern England and our performance during this period, we were told, booked us a place in the top bracket job of GHQ Signals. To my mind this was not surprising as we were, after all, employed daily in the business of telephones.

Towards the second week of manoeuvres we were told that we were on standby as it was touch and go whether the Second World War started now or a little later, but, as events turned out, it was to be the following September before we got our marching orders. War was declared on 3 September 1939 and by the middle of that month we were in France and billeted in a quaint little village called Dainville, just outside the historically famous town of Arras, which was now established as British Expeditionary Force GHQ. Our billet was in the local dance-hall, attached to the pub called Café l'Aeroplane, which was, of course, an excellent watering-hole for any of our troops who took a dram. They could really tank up and almost literally fall into bed. Needless to say, the troops made very good use of this facility. Being a non-drinker myself, I soon discovered that the cuisine side of the café was more interesting and that Madame made a wonderful omelette and chips which, strangely enough, never gave me a single headache or hangover!

Our unit had an outstanding reception in France as, apparently, we were the first complete outfit to arrive; at a very grand full-dress parade in the main square in Arras, we were presented with the flag of the Légion d'Honneur (I think). Before the ceremony took place we were warned there was to be no hilarity when the French officer kissed our officer on both cheeks, as this was only ceremonial and not affection. We were not convinced, but as the RSM had his beady eye on us, we behaved ourselves.

The weather was fantastic and we were amazed at the number of fruit trees that lined the highways and byways in our operational area. We seemed to be driving over apples everywhere we went that September.

We soon settled down to work in an area where, in the previous war, many huge battles had been fought. We ran lines over historic sites like Vimy Ridge and examined the old trenches which had been preserved to remind people of the horrors of the war which was fought to end wars. And here we were again, like a lot of kids, ready to do it all again. Unbelievable! How often will the politicians be allowed to sacrifice so many for the indulgence of so few? Why not follow the new government legislation and have a one-for-one ballot of the Electoral Register? I don't think we would need to be involved with any nuclear deterrents if we did that. How many mothers agree to their sons and daughters going off like animals to be maimed

4

or slaughtered? Unfortunately men think differently, or don't think enough, and this was seen in the number of volunteers in the Second World War who were men who had served in the First World War.

Aided by the Indian summer of '39, we began to spread our huge spider-like network of lines of communication over the HQ area. We never really had the feeling of being on active service and the odd German reconnaissance plane did little to remind us that there was a war on. Unfortunately, the winter that followed was unfit for brass monkeys, let alone us, and turned out to be the coldest ever recorded in that part of France. Our particular job became a daytime nightmare. As we did our work, our Section Officer, although unable to help us physically, plied us with tots of rum which helped to keep our blood circulating. At times it was so bad that the linemen were being roped so that they could be lowered if necessary from the pole they were working on to the ground when they could no longer climb down on their own.

We struggled on until spring arrived. Then came the aftermath of the big freeze. The winter frosts had bitten so deep that, when the thaw came, the frozen moisture began to expand and the cobbled roads boiled up like rising dough and became impassable, although they were centuries old and had withstood the traffic of everything from horse to tank. This was an impressive natural obstacle to add to the rest.

3

In early April I had a stroke of luck. I was picked to ride shotgun on one of our trucks doing a duty run to

Paris to collect some essentials for HQ. Naturally, I was asked to make some purchases of items which could not be obtained in the north – such as campbeds for Jimmy, Joe and myself, as we were fed-up sleeping on palliasses stuffed with straw. The Signals had a slight degree of leniency that would not have been tolerated in an infantry regiment.

Paris was, of course, out of bounds to all troops unless they were in possession of a pass. At this time everything in Paris looked fairly normal. Having only seen cities like Glasgow, Edinburgh and London, I was not quite sure what to expect, but Paris in the spring exceeded everything I could have imagined. We had only two days to absorb it all, but Driver McLean had done it all before so I got the whole guided tour. I managed to lose my virginity to a young mademoiselle. I even remembered to buy the campbeds.

On our return to Arras we heard rumours of the first rumblings of the German war machine. Confirmation was coming through that the German preparations were complete and they would soon be on the move. The French army were girding their loins, so to speak, on the impregnable Maginot Line and all forces were on Red Alert. The contention was, of course, that there would be no Blitzkrieg in France as there had been in Poland earlier. I wonder where one should apportion the blame for what was to follow. Should Belgium and Holland have agreed to an extension of the defence line, which would have made any real invasion a non-starter? The cost of such an undertaking was probably prohibitive, but would it not have been cheaper in the long run?

The Maginot Line became the Imaginary Line, and the Blitzkrieg came after all, but through Belgium instead of

France. When the breakthrough came, a Signal section was made up to establish communications from GHQ to the new front line using the French and Belgian telephone exchanges, which were rapidly being evacuated by their staff. Joe and I were part of this group but Jimmy was deployed to another detail. This was one of the few times that we were separated.

From Arras we linked up through Douai and then Tournai. By this time both towns were in flames and practically deserted as the Luftwaffe bombed and strafed the area almost unopposed. We were eventually stopped by our own troops, who kindly informed us that if we went any further on there would be no way back; they were blowing up the canal and river bridges as they retreated. A quick telephone call to HQ confirmed that we should get the hell out of it and return to our new coastal meeting point at Calais.

The roads were in a state of total turmoil on our way back. The gruesome scenes in the ditches – the dead lying where they had been thrown off the highway to make way for the traffic – should have disturbed us much more than they did. My personal lack of reaction to seeing men, women and, worst of all, children lying in a variety of death poses, like bundles of discarded clothing, surprised me very much indeed. I can only think that this was a subconscious protection of my sanity – that as long as we had no physical contact with the horrors we faced, we could not be adversely affected by them. The fact that all these people had proved to be mortal seemed only to enhance our own feeling of immortality.

Eventually we arrived in Boulogne, in the middle of a night bombing raid by the Luftwaffe. Hell had been let loose. The noise of the low-flying aircraft dropping bombs coupled with indiscriminate machine-gunning being answered by Bofors guns and anything else that could return fire created a real cacophony of soul-searing sound.

All this was, of course, taking place in a total black-out, with a huge conglomeration of traffic which slowly ground to a halt. The private car immediately behind us, for no apparent reason, switched on his headlights. This, quite rightly, brought roars of disapproval – as if a referee had refused a penalty claim at a Rangers/Celtic match. When the offending lights were not promptly doused, Jock McGregor vaulted over the tailboard of our truck and with the heels of his number ten tackety boots smashed both head-lamps, in all probability saving the lives of all in the vicinity of those telltale lights.

4

We finally reached our projected meeting place with the rest of our Section, only to find that they had been moved further up the coast, probably to Calais, possibly to Dunkirk – each soon to become household words. Our orders now were to stay overnight in the Rest Camp at Boulogne and to join up with our unit the following day. We found the camp. Oh, the luxury of a proper meal! Although the air-raid was still going on, we just bedded down where we were, too tired to even think of going to the air-raid shelter.

An uncomfortable awakening came with the dawn, but after a hard-tack breakfast we felt quite refreshed and looked forward to joining up with our own outfit. But it was not to be. The Gods of War had decided that our adventure was not quite finished and had devised a nasty, untidy ending for our little group.

Our special Signal Section was assembled and preparing to leave the Rest Camp when a staff car pulled in and a captain wearing a red arm band bustled out and called everyone to attention. A short speech informed us that all transit personnel were being commandeered for special duties; a light armoured German column had broken through our main front and was believed to be heading in our direction. We would be used to set up road blocks at strategic points outside the town. When the emergency was over we could return to our normal duties. In my case, this turned out to be over four years later.

Joe and I, along with a few odds and bods, were put under the command of a Royal Army Medical Corps captain, whose name I never knew. Nor did we know that this little job was a death sentence for him: very soon he was to die just a couple of yards from me.

His first instructions were to set up a road block in the village of La Capelle, just outside Boulogne on the St Omer road. As we travelled towards our destination everyone seemed fairly cheerful, until a most disturbing incident took place which changed our mood to one of gloom and despondency and set our mission in its true perspective. Our vehicles were flagged down just outside the town and, because we were obviously going in the wrong direction, we were asked if anyone wished to be given the last sacrament by an army chaplain. Even the Catholics declined this kind offer, which I can understand, because to accept it was to admit that our new mission was possibly terminal.

This stoppage also shed new light on my own position in the party. Prior to leaving the camp, the staff officer had asked if there were any good rifle shots among us. Knowing I was in that category, my hand went up without thinking. In doing so, I broke the first law I had been taught after putting on a uniform: 'volunteer for nothing'. The result of my unthinking action was that I had to relinquish my rifle and take a bren gun in its place. After fiddling with it for a few minutes I was able to see how the bolt action worked and the magazine could be changed. I never dreamed that I would be called upon to use it. Volunteers usually get the heavy end of the stick, as in the case where a section sergeant asked if he could have six men who were interested in music and the men who responded had to shift a grand piano, which probably resulted in at least a couple of hernias. That damned bren gun was to get me into a lot of trouble very soon.

When we reached La Capelle there were all the usual routines to follow. Setting up a local HQ, finding a suitable place for the cookhouse, a place to bed down, latrine position and, of paramount importance, the siting of the road-block.

All sorts of ideas went through our minds as to how one would go about blocking a road, but the staff captain who was still with us at this stage had decided on a very simple method. You make up your mind where you want the rear of the road-block and then you stop all the traffic coming from the danger zone and place these vehicles crosswise on the road. There would be no exceptions.

That sounds simple until you see the people you are forcing to leave their vehicles: the old and infirm, pregnant mothers, cripples, nuns and so on. They all had valid reasons for not leaving the security of their transport, but their pleas fell on deaf ears. Any men of military age were escorted to the rear to be questioned, and if their answers did not satisfy the commanding officer, they were summarily dealt with behind the HQ barn. This was to avoid the possibility of infiltration by the Fifth Column.

5

Wars are remembered by famous actions and battles, for example the Battle of Hastings, where Harold took an arrow in the eye and made it easy for schoolchildren to remember him. Another example is the Charge of the Light Brigade, where almost everyone was gloriously and famously killed. Let's not forget Nelson being fatally wounded or what he said to Hardy as he died. All these and many other historical actions faded into insignificance for us when compared with 'The Battle of La Capelle', which was about to take place.

The scene was set – our road block completed, traffic had dried up and one of those wartime phenomena took place for which these is no explanation. As if acting on a signal, the householders of the village came out and closed their shutters, top and bottom.

At this point, only Jimmy Strathearn and myself were at the front of the road block. I had to stop the German army with my bren gun and he had to carry the ammunition and keep me supplied with fresh magazines. The bren was sited in the middle of the road, with an ammunition box on either side, facing in the direction from which we expected the trouble to come. A hundred yards in front the road took a turn to the left and an empty car stood on the corner. Jimmy and I were discussing the strange behaviour of the villagers and wondering what it meant when the sound of a small plane caught our attention.

A few seconds later a single-engined monoplane approached us, flying fairly low. Seeing the black crosses on the underside of the wings, we realised that we were in the presence of the enemy. It was obviously a reconnaissance plane and offered no personal threat to us, but to Jimmy this was a chance to do battle and he insisted I 'shoot the bloody thing down'. I pointed out that the bren had a very low tripod and that unless the pilot flew at road level there was nothing much I could do. But Jimmy was not to be denied and insisted I use his shoulder as a high tripod. As I was quite keen to see if I had figured out the working of the gun properly, we did just that. These planes fly very slowly, which is just as well, otherwise this one would have been gone by the time we got organised. With Jimmy holding the tripod on his shoulder, I released the safety-catch, worked a round into the breach, aimed – allowing for speed – then squeezed the trigger.

Then came all the things that gave me satisfaction in shooting: the noise – which accounts for my being almost totally deaf in my right ear – the smell of cordite and the feel of the tightly-held gun butt bouncing on the shoulder. As I wasn't using tracers I couldn't tell how close I came but, judging by the pilot's reaction, it must have been good because he was off like a bat out of hell. Jimmy was jubilant, picked up one of the spent cartridge cases and put it in my pocket as a souvenir. He then decided he had seen some movement in an adjacent field and went off to investigate. He had just disappeared when the captain came forward to find out what the shooting was all about. When I told him, he decided to stay forward in case I needed any help. I had no idea how the others were deployed but it seemed awfully lonely up front.

Suddenly all hell broke loose. There was one huge bang and the car on the corner blew apart. Shrapnel zizzed all around us. It was obviously suspected of being an observation post and was completely wiped out. The captain and myself dropped to the ground, still in the middle of the road behind the bren. Before we could say anything, there was a loud rumbling and round the corner came one very large tank displaying a black cross on its turret. Fortunately, it stopped to survey the situation and gave me time to line up my sights on the driver's sight slit and to fire a burst from the bren. The captain had decided that our position was too exposed. The tank commander must have decided that we were no great threat to them but had given us the few seconds necessary to get off the road and into the nearest garden.

This is where fate took a hand in the proceedings. Opening the garden gate, the officer turned right and took up position with the rifle he was carrying, leaving me no option but to turn left and take position there with the bren. We didn't have long to wait. The tank rumbled towards us and took station just outside the garden. My mind was racing with the possibilities of what would happen next. I figured that the turret lid would open and a hand grenade would be slung into the garden, so I held the bren so that I could fire a burst at the lid to discourage them. Sure enough the turret began to swivel and I thought I had been right. My finger tightened on the trigger and I waited for the lid to open. Instead, the tank's machine gun raked through the garden. Shocked at being on the receiving end of gunfire for the first time in my life, I saw the captain's head sag as the burst hit him across the back. Then it was my turn. I was hit by lightning in my left leg. I remember thinking that a second burst would finish me off and my poor mother would never know what had happened to me, but it never came.

As the tank moved off I had a chance to evaluate the situation. My leg was completely numb; blood was oozing out of a wound in the ankle and this seemed to be the main damage, although about a week later a bullet was discovered lodged in my thigh bone. I checked the bren and found that a ricochet had damaged the breech, which also accounted for the blood on my left hand. The mopping-up troops were now visible through the hedge. A few minutes later I could have been finished off by the big German sergeant who came into the garden behind his threatening Luger. I closed my eyes as I didn't want to see the shot that killed me, but when I heard him shouting at me I opened them again. He was motioning for me to stand up. I pointed to my bloody ankle and shook my head, whereupon he went to the door of the house and hammered on it with the butt of his automatic.

When the door was opened he went in and reappeared carrying a chair, which he placed on the path near me. Then, with very little apparent effort, he picked me up and gently placed me on it. He then checked the bren and, on finding that the bolt was jammed, unceremoniously threw it in a corner. Opening one of his tunic pockets, he produced a packet of cigarettes and offered me one. When I indicated that I didn't smoke, he courteously offered me a bar of chocolate out of the other pocket. To this I said 'Thank you, but no thank you'. He now went into one of his trouser pockets and produced a field dressing; after removing the gaiter, boot and sock from my damaged ankle, he bandaged it. Everything was done with great care and consideration, yet the same man could just as easily have killed me and no-one would have been any the wiser. All very confusing.

He now did his level best to interrogate me as to the deployment of troops in the area. I don't think there could have been a less informed person than I. After he established that I belonged to the Signal Corps and not an infantry regiment, he relieved me of my pride and joy – my lovely chrome pliers which I carried in a holster on my belt.

This big gentle man then arranged transport to take me to the nearest German field hospital, where I was placed in a long queue awaiting field surgery. The real war had broken out down beyond our road block, with lots of different kinds of gunfire. Finally the Stukas were called in to dive-bomb the obstruction to the German advance.

About a year later Joe told me the rest of the La Capelle story. Apparently the lead tank which shot us went on down the road and straight over the road block as if it wasn't there, firing its machine-gun as it went. Joe said he had never seen our group move so fast as they dispersed towards the coast. He eventually met up with my brother Jimmy, who wanted to come back and look for me. The squad convinced him that I must have been killed and that there was no way back. The official verdict was 'Missing believed killed in action'. So ended my one and only go at fighting in the war.

6

After a succession of dressing stations and hospitals I finally ended up in the British 21st Field Hospital in the town of Camiers. Although a British hospital, it was under German control. The hospital itself was under the command of Colonel Robertson, whose house I had worked in just before the war during the auto telephone conversion of the area he lived in. This connection was a stroke of luck.

I had been told I would never have full use of my ankle again and would probably need calipers to walk. At the hospital, however, there was Colonel Wilson, a brilliant surgeon, and Major Tucker, an outstanding bone specialist, both reputed to have practices in Harley Street. They decided that I should be able to use my ankle again, and after a great deal of pain and time this objective was achieved. Years later I was re-graded in an army medical and passed A1. It is strange to think that if I had not been channelled through this hospital I would very likely have been crippled for the rest of my life.

A few months later, a group of us who were just able to hobble about were assembled and put into a variety of French, Belgian and British uniforms and unceremoniously bundled into a freight wagon, whose doors were slammed and bolted. We spent three miserable days and nights in this hell-hole as the train was slowly shunted to Upper Silesia in Eastern Germany, close to the Polish border. Occasionally the doors were opened and some rations thrown in, but we were never allowed to get out. Someone enterprisingly ripped up a piece of the floor and this served as our toilet for the trip. I often have a quiet giggle to myself when I hear people complaining about the terrible inconveniences that they have had to put up with.

Eventually we reached our destination and were rousted out with lots of noise and shouting. To my horror, my walking stick, a necessity rather than an affectation, was taken from me and thrown aside, as were all the crutches and sticks of the group. We made a sorry spectacle as we shambled through the town, sore from the discomfort of our trip and unable to walk properly. We were not a pretty sight. The townsfolk must have wondered why the war was taking so long; if we were an example of the British armed forces then the Hitler Youth should have been capable of wiping us out without the might of the Wehrmacht.

After this degrading march, we were transported by trucks to Stalag VIIIB, Lamsdorf, where we were body-searched and then lined up. There were already thousands of British prisoners in this main camp and, of course, a batch of new arrivals created quite a stir, with people checking to see if any of their friends or buddies were amongst them. It just so happened that Joe was one of those. When he recognised me, he was quite overcome, and after an emotional reunion he told me not to go away as he had another surprise for me – my brother Jimmy. Apparently when he told Jimmy that I was there Jimmy grabbed him by the throat and said that if this was a joke it was in very bad taste. This was understandable, as he had come to accept I had been killed at the road block. After much persuasion, Jimmy came along to see for himself, and once again our trio was complete.

Jimmy managed to convince the guards that we were brothers and I was allowed to stay with them in the same hut. There then followed for me a welcome period of recuperation, during which Jimmy and Joe did everything possible to get me back in shape. I began to realise that, given time, I would be able to walk normally again. You can imagine the stories we had to tell each other. After having been separated and captured in different places, it was an amazing coincidence to be re-united in the same Stalag in Eastern Germany.

I was now an official POW and had my own number to prove it. My mother was notified accordingly, whereupon she wrote to Winston Churchill that he should take it upon himself to see that I was provided with proper footwear so that I could make a full recovery. Astonishingly, as a result, an extra pair of new boots was delivered to me every six months through the Red Cross, outwith the normal issue. I often wonder what would have happened if she had insisted that I be repatriated immediately.

7

It was now catching-up time. Jimmy and Joe related their hair-raising adventures of how they had met again and been rounded up in the fort in Calais. They had no hope of being rescued from the beach there as the main retreat flotilla was concentrating on Dunkirk.

They and thousands of our other troops, still bewildered by the speed of events over the last few days and totally stunned by the outcome of the Blitzkrieg, were forced to march across France into Germany. This journey left scars on the minds of all those who took part in it and was always referred to afterwards as The March. No rations or drinking water were provided, and sleeping accommodation was simply the ground where they stopped for the night. Toilets were non-existent. This became a great problem as stomachs rebelled at what was being put into them – stagnant water from ponds and brooks, along with anything that looked edible. Naturally, all this took its toll and left them severely debilitated. We had been in reserved occupations at home and had, after all, volunteered. Nowadays when I see the commercials urging young men to join the Territorial Army, I feel they should be shown some of the horrors of war as well as the entertaining side of the army.

Over the next few years the amateur POWs arrived at the various Stalags which had been set up in Germany and Poland and, through bitter experience, became hardened professionals. Most of them had some untapped abilities of which they had not previously been aware. In their new life of enforced captivity there was time to think, listen, watch and learn – to try something new, to improvise and maybe succeed. Those who did not adjust to the new way of life became 'Stalag Happy' and lost touch with reality. Thank God this didn't happen to many of them.

Jimmy and Joe were first-class survivors and worked very well together. When they arrived in Stalag VIIIB, they organised themselves into the plum job in the camp – the cookhouse. In no time after my appearance in camp, I also was elected to a post on this elite staff.

Now began a period of readjustment for everyone. No-one could possibly forecast how long we were going to be 'in the bag', and everyone was well aware that it had been said that World War One would be over by Christmas. We realised that it might be years more before it was over, so the word was 'settle down, chaps, and make the best of it'. This having been established, the organisers took over.

Slowly the birds of a feather flocked together. The music men found a place where they could talk shop and make plans; likewise the bookworms, the artisans and others who had similar interests. As time went on the German authorities co-operated as far as possible in providing instruments for the musicians, and books and writing materials for the studious; eventually there were bands and various types of learning classes leading to examination standards which were accepted at home.

There were, of course, the Escape Committees which no self-respecting camp should be without. One of the unwritten laws states that it is a POW's duty to escape from the enemy and that, if successful, he will not be returned to the same theatre of war. One presumes this is so that he can go through the whole bloody business again, only under different conditions.

The Escape Committee is a weird and wonderful organisation for which there are no known qualifications – they don't exist in the real world. This means anyone in the camp is eligible to become a member. Many escapes were made as there was a hard core of men who made escaping their full-time occupation, even though they were captured time and again. These were the ones that the Committee delighted in concentrating on. A first-time escapee would be told that beginners could not receive assistance. This was what happened to us when we made our one and only approach for help.

We three discussed the pros and cons of escape and decided that in the first year it would be impossible, as I had to rebuild strength and mobility in my shattered ankle. A prime requirement for such a venture is physical fitness. It is strange, however, how the mind works. During the next few years we listened carefully to any stories we heard of where the escapes went wrong and a pattern began to build up: the same mistakes were being made time and again. They kept trying to travel at night and, as there was a curfew on, they were easily picked up. Some contacted the Polish people for help and almost always were turned over to the Germans. Subconsciously, this type of information was filed for future reference.

The camp slowly assumed the identity of a small town and in time the layout became familiar to everyone. If you wanted to go shopping you went to the swap-shop area, where it was possible to barter one thing for another. In the beginning, the trading was fairly primitive, but as time went on it became more and more interesting, especially after the Red Cross parcels began to arrive.

On a good day you could take a walk up to the Canadian compound and enjoy hearing a change of accent or, if you were feeling naughty, you might slowly pass the Married Quarters compound, which always led to a heated debate about the problems of homosexuality. Thank heaven we didn't have AIDS to worry about in those days. The energetic could congregate at the football field and perhaps get a game. The less energetic could always watch. Quite often it was worth watching as many good players had been captured, including a number of professionals.

You could visit Johnny the Barber and get your hair trimmed. If you were lucky there might be a cup of tea thrown in. After a tidy-up, a visit could be made to the theatre area, where one of the bands might be practising a piece worth listening to. Failing all else, you could just sit around and talk about your favourite food and drink, which, considering the circumstances, was a pretty stupid thing to do – but it was indulged in with great gusto and relish. It certainly made a contrast with our daily diet of soup, three or four potatoes and three hundred grams of bread.

Writing about it may make it sound like a holiday camp, but there were drawbacks – barbed wire and armed guards, for example. The limitation on movement was the real soul destroyer. This was what drove men in the main camp to volunteer for working parties.

8

After a desperately hard winter, in which we experienced the biting cold east winds from the Russian steppes blowing straight through us, came the slow miserable, messy Silesian spring. The warmer weather brought the terrible affliction of 'itchy feet'. This was our first spring in prison camp so we had no precedent to compare it with, but as the years went by it became something to look forward to, wondering who it was going to strike and how it would affect them. There were those who began to huddle and plan escapes which never came to fruition, and others who wondered how to wangle themselves onto the repatriation list. Others decided to go out on a working party or to switch to a different one. It was like the restlessness nowadays when winter turns the corner, only our options were rather more restricted – no dithering between Majorca, the Costa Brava or Bournemouth.

Jimmy, Joe and I had a long and serious talk about the importance of the next step. Should we give up our cosy jobs in the cookhouse and gamble on one of the working parties? We could end up regretting our decision for the rest of the war. Eventually we decided to give it a go and volunteered to go out as replacements on an existing working party. We got a right kick in the teeth.

We ended up in a railway construction job on the Polish border: a more desolate area would be hard to imagine. I can't remember what kind of working party we were supposed to be joining, but the lure was usually that you were told you were going to a chocolate or jam factory, which invariably turned out to be something completely different and horrible. There were a number of other parties in the area and we were warned that when the overall control officer visited the camp and gave an order, we should obey it as fast as possible. He turned out to be a German Army Sergeant Major and obviously the job had gone to his head. He was so brutal that he achieved a place on the Black List back home. His nickname 'the Killer' was given to him after two recaptured escapees were brought back to their camp where, in front of the other prisoners, he prodded and goaded them until one of them retaliated – whereupon he shot them in cold blood.

The work was hard and heavy. Handling the rail sleepers was back-breaking, with no machinery or equipment to help. Everything was done by muscle power, which wasn't easy on our type of rations. One consolation of this gruesome period was that we had never been so fit or healthy. I don't suppose it is so surprising, since we had no drink, drugs or fornication to upset our systems. Without fail, we were early to bed and early to rise. With our regular but limited diet, there wasn't a pot belly or spare tyre to be seen anywhere.

As soon as it was humanly possible we transferred out of this hell-hole. There followed a couple of other working parties, none of which could be recommended for food or accommodation. We soon realised that something was wrong, and the three of us sat down to work it out. We realised that we were operating at the wrong rank level: the answer to our job problem was that we would have to have Stalag promotions and become NCOs. So Jimmy was to be made a Sergeant and Joe and I would be made up to Corporals. This proved surprisingly easy. We were allowed to write a certain number of postcards home and we used them to tell our families to start using our new ranks when sending us mail, which they duly did. Slowly the new ranks became accepted and in time both the German authorities and we grew used to them. One of the advantages was that NCOs could, if on a working party, ask at any time to return to the main camp.

In 1942 we decided that we had done our share of work in the hard labour camps and that it was time to test our stripes, remembering of course that they were self-awarded and only on our uniforms. We duly applied for a transfer back to Stalag VIIIB and were quite astounded when we were returned without question.

9

The three of us were in agreement about the strangeness of being back in total captivity again. On a working party you are almost out in the normal world, although not actually part of it, whereas in the main camp you suffer total segregation, which is a punishment that no one in their right mind would want. It was in Stalags like ours that the abbreviation BEF took on a new meaning. Properly, it stood for British Expeditionary Force, but to the fifty thousand left behind by Lord 'Tiger' Gort, it now meant the Bastards England Forgot. It proves the adage that if you're stupid enough to get caught, then you must take the consequences, and that was exactly what we were doing. Next time we would be off like a shot and to hell with the barricades.

We circulated around camp for about three weeks renewing our contacts with Signal associates and all the other friends we had made in the last two years. They were glad to see us and there were interminable 'bumming schools' as we brought them up to date about what happened to us on the outside. They, in turn, filled us in on the latest intrigues in camp, and so a few more hours dribbled through the time machine in this game of waiting for release.

But all good things come to an end and we began to attend to the purpose of our return to camp, namely to find a good NCO working party where we could live happily ever after. We were delighted to hear that twenty NCOs were required for a holiday village in the mountains. All the able-bodied men there had now been drafted into the army and the local jobs had to be filled to keep things going. To us it sounded very much like the old chocolate factory story, but there was only one way to find out if it was true. So we put our names down and were accepted – but for what?

About a week later our party was mustered and with all our worldly possessions in a bag we moved out, after having said our farewells again to everyone; parting in those days was often terminal.

It was a short trip from the camp to the railway station and by the time we were on the train we knew we were on our way to a place called Bad Karlsbrunn, which was indeed a holiday village in Sudetenland. We had heard many stories before the war about this country, which originally had been part of Czechoslovakia and later was colonised by the Germans, but we knew little of its real history. To me the name Sudetenland was a just a name like Persia, Albania or California – exotic places which I knew existed but were unlikely ever to be part of my world. Yet here we were on our way to a place which for two years became a real 'Shangri La'.

As the train laboured slowly southward away from the Silesian industrial belt, the landscape improved with every mile that we travelled until, on the horizon, the foothills and mountains of the Altvater range became visible.

You cannot imagine our feelings as the scenery became more and more like Scotland. The last part of the journey by bus from the railhead at Wurbenthal to Bad Karlsbrunn was a steady climb through the forest and halfway up the mountain. Finally, we reached our camp, which was sited at the side of the River Oppa, over two thousand feet above sea level.

10

The number one man in our Bad Karlsbrunn working party was Sergeant Bill James – a famous surname you will remember from the main members of the notorious 'James Gang', namely Frank and Jesse. They were reputedly the toughest outlaws who ever lived but, believe me, they would have been regarded as sissies compared with our Bill.

I first met him when we were both hospitalised after being wounded. He had suffered a nasty shrapnel wound which had cut across the Achilles tendon on one leg. For a while we were in the same boat, having to learn to walk again. He must have heard that I was a Scot and, having become mobile before me, became a regular visitor and taught me many card tricks, which I still produce to amuse and amaze my grandchildren. He was a very good friend and looked after my interests while I was immobilised. But I had no idea then what a tough cookie he really was.

Bill was born and reared in the Vale of Leven and boasted that there was only one person in the world who could get the better of him physically – someone who could actually punch harder and faster than him. Having seen him in action many times in the years that I knew him, I had to ask who this man was. Without a blush, Bill admitted that it was his beloved mother.

It became apparent in the course of time that he had a strong aversion to bullies and braggarts. If anyone tried to throw their weight around, he always had to take them on and the result was inevitable, with the victim wondering how this eleven-stone pale-faced man could administer such punishment. Putting his knuckles back to where they should be after these bouts was always a problem, but they always healed in time to deal with the next offender.

Other Scots in the party, apart from Jimmy, Joe and myself, were Big John, Mully Mitchell, Phony and Young Alec. We also had two Kiwis and a genuine Maori, one Aussie, three Merchant Navy lads, one Air Force Brylcream boy and the rest a mixture of army units, which included Busty Waring of the Royal Artillery. Busty was the type you see at the Earls Court display lifting gun barrels and wheels over walls, so you know exactly how he looked. With it he was always bright and bouncy. Our Maori was called Charlie, and a more lovable character I have yet to meet, with a good singing voice and the ability to accompany himself on the guitar. When he sang the Maori farewell song 'Now is the Hour', it was a very touching moment for everyone, though we didn't often indulge in the luxury of sentiment. Charlie's singing always made me reflect on what a hard-bitten crew we had become.

The personality mix of our party was intriguing. For instance, take our two Kiwis, who could not have been more conflicting in character – Jim Rowe was the perfect laconic colonial, who didn't sit on a chair but managed always to drape himself over it, perfectly relaxed, whereas his oppo, Davey Jay, was always ready to move at any given moment and, when he sat down, was like a coiled spring waiting to be released. Jim was blond and slim and sported a moustache, whereas Davey was clean-shaven and dark, slightly smaller and thick-set. Davey had been a fairly competent boxer at home, which, at a later date, almost cost him his life – it certainly cost him his sanity.

Mully Mitchell, or to give him his full title, Motherwell Mitchell, was a cheery dapper little Scot who was a friend of Bill James – another of the Argylls who had been left behind to fight the thankless rearguard action. Mully on the football field was every bit as good as Bill in a fist-fight, but his greatest forte was as a naturalist. He showed me how to capture wild birds, examine them without hurting them and then release them. I had heard of the art of tickling trout but Mully was the first person to demonstrate it before my very eyes, again returning the fish unharmed to the river. He was a real charmer.

Our tame Australian was called Arthur and was a nice-looking bundle of raw muscle. To this day I can't make up my mind if most of his stories were boastful truth or sheer romancing. I didn't care as they were very entertaining, like the one he told us about the time he was driving a four-horse harvester in the wheat fields. The story goes that his team-mate on the other harvester hurt himself and a replacement couldn't be found in time to complete the contract. But all was not lost. Arthur had the brilliant idea of making a special rig so that he could drive the two harvesters and the eight-horse team by himself. If Arthur had said that the horses were slowing down and that eventually he had to pull the harvesters himself, I would have applauded him loudly.

Brother Jimmy had been a godsend over the last two years in all the camps we had lived in, as he had an almost phobic tendency towards cleanliness and keeping things tidy. He had imposed his strong will in this direction no matter how much opposition there was. Some of the squalor we encountered was quite unbelievable, but when we left a camp behind, thanks to Jimmy, it was always cleaner than when we arrived.

Not many POWs had the good fortune to have a big brother to look after them in such circumstances, and to think he was there because of me made me feel terribly guilty at times. Jimmy should have been at home working in his nice reserved occupation with a perfectly clear conscience, but when I decided to join the Reserves he re-enlisted to help me through the first couple of years. His reward for this brotherly love was four years behind barbed wire, doomed to spend the whole of the war away from his beloved wife.

The deprivation that the married men suffered was naturally more acute than that of the single men, and quite often I could see the effects of it on both Joe and Jimmy. Being such strong characters, they came through these spells with flying colours. On the other hand, the bachelors reverted to the roving eye technique, which was, of course, possible when you were out on a working party where you could look and let your mind wander. During the first two years in Silesia most of the female temptresses were dressed in oily boiler suits and were built like tanks. This wasn't surprising as they were doing the jobs of their absent husbands who had worked in the engine sheds and railway yards before being drafted, and only the strongest type of female could survive.

11

The camp was a wooden structure surrounded by a high barbed wire fence put there, I suppose, to protect us from wild animals or anything else that might harm us. It certainly wasn't there to keep us in, or if it was, it didn't work. We couldn't see the village from our compound; we were just around the corner from the main street and very close to the local farm.

Before we ever set eyes on the village, the question of allocation of jobs had to be settled. Jimmy pulled a job in the Spa bath-house, Joe became an assistant to the joiner and I became a plasterer's labourer – a fine re-allocation of three technicians.

Our bosses were supposed to wear armbands, showing them to be assistant guards. Their job was to collect us each morning and return us to the camp in the evening when we finished work, but both the armbands and the collection idea were soon given up and we were trusted to appear and disappear on time.

The plastering team consisted of the boss, one Herr Springer, who was an uncommunicative fifty-year-old with a bad tummy, and his number two, ragdoll character called Franz, who had lost all his toes in World War One and consequently walked strangely. He was also one of the nicest men I have ever met. When Springer wasn't around, Franz took it upon himself to try and teach me some German. He was so successful that years later I was asked where on earth I had learned such hillbilly German.

Bad Karlsbrunn itself is a small mountain spa village with healing peat baths and special spring water, which tasted awful but reputedly was good for the innards. If this was true, then why did Herr Springer suffer so much? The main business was the baths and all the rest was hotels, ranging from the top-class down to the ordinary ski hotels. The type of skiing was fairly restricted as there were no ski lifts of any kind and the only skiers around were the local children, who were very good and exciting to watch. This was hardly surprising as they started to ski as soon as they could walk. The slopes were also used by the German army and formed a training area for mountain troops.

Most of the residents in the village were involved in the holiday business, which was why the village existed. There were only a few shops on the main street, such as the butcher, the baker and the shop that sold everything, including souvenirs. In the beginning the locals were quite stand-offish. This was hardly surprising, since we were the enemy: all they knew about the British Tommies was what they had been fed through the powerful German propaganda machine. Suddenly here were twenty of them in their midst. Fortunately for us, we had now been supplied with new battledress and everyone looked smart and tidy. Those who wished also acquired shorts and shirts for summer wear, which looked great with our all-weather tans. As time passed the villagers realised we were successfully doing the jobs we had come to do. The general attitude became more relaxed and we began to blend into the scenery – so much so that some of the visitors who didn't know we were POWs would nod, smile and even pass the time of day, thinking probably we were members of the Pioneer Group of the Organisation Tod, whose dress was very similar to ours.

By now all the female talent in the village had been spotted, discussed and placed in order of desirability, which was, of course, only a mental exercise which could never be realised under our present circumstances. But, as they say in the song, you can't stop people from dreaming, no matter how you guard them. Some orientals say that the pattern of our life is made like a tapestry and cannot be altered. Some people disagree and say that if you look closely you can see where there are options to take a path less travelled. Here in Karlsbrunn I had a choice between having an easy life or one fraught with danger. This is what happened.

It was midsummer and all was right with the world. I was enjoying the physical labour of mixing cement and sand in front of one of the hotels where Franz and I were repairing the stairway and, as I stopped for a breather, caught sight of a blond mädchen watching me from one of the hotel windows. She was leaning on the window-sill and the sunlight was doing wonderful things to her hair. I looked away and then back again. Sure enough, she was still watching me and there was a hint of a smile on her face which looked quite lovely. Although this was only visual contact, it was, nonetheless, extremely exciting, and mixing the proper quantities of sand and cement became of secondary importance. I returned what I hoped was a smile in her direction and this time her smile was unmistakable and definitely for me. Palpitations now set in, and I knew it wasn't sunstroke. When I looked up at the window again, the vision had vanished and now I wondered if I had really seen anything at all. Had I finally succumbed to frustration and joined the 'Stalag Happy' brigade?

That evening I told Jimmy about the incident. In his wisdom he gave me various pieces of advice on how to deal the situation. The main theme was to exercise extreme caution, as the penalty for fraternisation with the enemy during hostilities was execution of both parties. The best thing would be to forget the whole thing had ever happened. He also said that if the young lady was a visitor to the hotel, she would soon leave. This was a possibility that I hadn't thought of, and it didn't appeal to me at all. Jimmy was right: proceed with caution and don't make any fast moves.

Next day I could hardly wait to get into the village. We were still working at the same hotel and the only thought in my mind was 'would I see her again?' or had the bird already flown? The question was answered in the afternoon when she suddenly appeared from the rear door pushing a pram. This really set me back. Obviously she was a young married woman with a baby and her husband was fighting on the Eastern Front – or somewhere else – but she had more or less flirted with me the day before. How could she? But maybe that was all rubbish and it was her little sister or brother. Or maybe she was baby-sitting. When she spotted me staring at her, she stopped and fussed a bit with the baby, then straightened up and subjected me to that happy smile again. I was devastated to say the least. In her mountain dirndl she looked a real picture. I was in love.

In my return smile, I tried to say everything that I felt, but probably managed only to look soppy. Then she moved slowly away towards the village. It took me about a week to find out who she was and about another week to find out her name. Remembering Jimmy's advice about being circumspect, I found it difficult to ask questions without raising suspicions. For now, let us call her Traudl. She was the daughter of the caretaker couple in the hotel where I first saw her.

My German course with Franz now took on a new urgency

and importance. I knew that if by any chance I ever made contact with Traudl, questions and answers would have to be dealt with in German. I worked hard on my side. I obtained a German/English dictionary and set myself the task of memorising two or three new words every day. For me, this was a considerable undertaking, but I had a powerful incentive to study – conversing with Traudl.

12

The mood in our working party was extremely high. The pleasant surroundings were to our liking. After the horrors of Upper Silesia, this was a veritable holiday camp. After two years of misery, we were all set to enjoy the pleasant quirk of fate that had placed us here. There was not a single complaint about any member of the party not giving satisfaction on the jobs they were doing. Our food from the Kur Hotel was satisfactory and the Red Cross parcels supplemented our diet nicely. So what more could a body want?

Take twenty men, feed them, make them fit, lock them up every night after work and what have you got? Big trouble. All those healthy hormones being generated – and what do you tell them? Forget it and go to sleep? Unfortunately, hormones don't listen.

The German army guards were very understanding and allowed us to play football on a piece of spare ground adjacent to the camp as there wasn't enough room in our compound. On Sundays we would play for two or three hours at a time. Those who didn't want to play or watch were locked in the camp while the guards supervised the game. Football helped us to get rid of some surplus energy, but the underlying problem remained. The rooftop demonstrations we have nowadays in our prisons, the fights with wardens, prisoners taking hostages and other types of misconduct all stem from the same source – over-active hormones.

Some of the lads were working near a group of Greek girls in the village and found them quite receptive to their advances. There was, of course, no possibility of any contact with them during the day, even though the ladies indicated where their living quarters were. So began the first talks in the barracks of how to get out of the camp at night and, more importantly, how to get back in safely. Everyone agreed that a bolt-hole was a good idea, even if it was never used. The problem was to get from our bungalow into the compound without using any of the windows or doors. After a lot of discussion, a decision was reached which met with everyone's approval: using an existing trap-door in the floor of the kitchen. When we lifted the lid, it exposed a cavity under the floor about three feet deep, lined with wood, which had obviously been a cold store. Our planning experts removed the wood from the end nearest the wall and made a tunnel which came up through the floor of the outside toilet in the compound.

It sounds simple, but it wasn't easy to conceal. When it was finished, it was a first-class job and quite undetectable. The wooden floor in the outside toilet was also doctored. It became a lid which could be lifted and replaced easily when you knew how to do it. This made a good vantage point for checking whether it was safe to approach the barbed-wire perimeter fence, part of which could be lifted sufficiently above ground level to allow someone to crawl through, closing the wire behind him.

It was agreed that the use of the tunnel would be under the supervision of Bill James, who would decide when it was safe to use it and how many could go on the same night. It was also agreed that the tunnel would never be used for an escape 'for real'. In all working parties there was an unwritten rule that no-one should escape from a good camp, the proper procedure being to return to the main camp and then choose a camp where conditions would not be jeopardised by an escape. Shortly after its completion, another use was found for the mole-hole.

We were contacted by an escapee from another camp and agreed to put him up for one night. We asked a million questions, but his stock answer was: did we not get all this information from our radio? We didn't have a radio but it was then agreed that we should try to acquire one. The think-tank went into operation. We knew that if a radio was stolen anywhere in the surrounding area we would be the prime suspects, so we would have to go further afield. But how could we pinpoint a target in a strange mountain area? I finally came up with a possible solution. On odd occasions when I wasn't needed by the plasterers, I was used by the local van driver on trips to buy provisions for the village. This meant travelling to the nearest town, where we usually indulged in the luxury of an ersatz coffee at a gasthaus; on the sideboard of its sitting room lived a large radio.

It was agreed that the distance from the camp was about right to avoid suspicion, but could we cover the ten miles there and back, partly on the road and partly cross-country in the dark, lugging a heavy radio? Was it really a viable proposition, how many men would we need, when would we set out and how long would it take us? Every question required careful thought as our lives would depend on getting the answers correct. It was agreed that the prize was worth the effort. The next step was picking the team and setting the date, the latter being dependent on the weather, which would have to be good.

I would have to go, as I was the only one who knew the way; Bill decided he would be another and that he would make the entry with me and bring the set out. Another four stalwarts would be needed to cover us when we were inside. They would also be able to share the carrying of the radio back to camp. Jimmy was an automatic choice as one of the four, which made me feel a lot safer; we had a mutual understanding which did not require words and almost amounted to thought transference.

Such an undertaking showed the state of our minds after three years of war. In peacetime the whole idea would have seemed reprehensible, but here we were happily planning and discussing breaking, entering and stealing.

13

Almost every working day now I saw Traudl somewhere in the village. In my heart I believed she went out of her way to make this possible. On my side, if a day went by without my seeing her I felt it was wasted. Then fate stepped in and the pace quickened. Herr Springer told the guard that they would be away on a certain day and could they please arrange for me to have some gainful employment elsewhere. I wasn't very pleased about this until I heard where it was: the basement of the hotel where Traudl lived. The job was to pick out the bad potatoes from the good ones in the hotel cellar cold store – a real stinker of a job in more ways than one, especially for a fresh air fiend like myself.

But this time I was more than happy to take on the chore. To have the chance of perhaps meeting the lady of my dreams gave me quite a tingle and also a chance to work on my thought transference technique. I have always believed in telepathy and on this particular day it worked like a charm. So if you ever want to try it, make sure you have some smelly potatoes around. Within an hour of my arrival in the cellar there was the patter of feet coming down the stairs from the hotel. There she was – Traudl with a basket over her arm for the family's ration of potatoes.

Can you imagine the odds against such a situation? For a POW on a working party suddenly to find himself alone with the girl of his dreams, with no-one around to disturb or distract them, was quite amazing. Yet that is exactly what happened.

Traudl looked very surprised to see someone in the cellar, but when she saw it was me she gave me a big wide-eyed smile of recognition, which I happily returned. The next ten minutes were taken up with introducing ourselves, at first very tentatively, but a rapport quickly built up between us and ended with my suggesting we meet some night after dark at the edge of the woods near the hotel. She was naturally a bit sceptical about the idea but I worked hard at convincing her that I could do it and in the end she agreed. I was shocked at how limited my German was and decided to work much harder with my little dictionary. The strange thing is that if I had been in the main Stalag in Lamsdorf I could have taken a real first-class course in German under a proper teacher. On the other hand if I had been in the main camp there would have been no incentive to learn the language.

Three of the lads had already tried out the tunnel outlet a few times to visit the Greek girls at their quarters in the village. However, the strain had become so great on them that their outings became fewer and eventually died out altogether, they having decided in favour of a quiet and peaceful life. I confided in Joe and Jimmy about my proposed meeting with Traudl: they both agreed that I must be crackers to attempt such a thing, but they would give me all the help I needed. Dress was very important, nothing white or reflective, and shoes would have to be covered over with an old pair of socks to reduce noise to a minimum. The route I would take was worked out between the three of us and I was warned that after clearing the camp lights I would have to stop and wait until my eyes re-adjusted to the darkness.

I told Bill about my date and he wished me luck and said that I would be out on my own that night, which suited me fine as I had no wish to bump into any of my own pals. I was reminded by Bill that there was a curfew on, and if I got into trouble outside it would be disaster for the whole camp. So at all costs I must avoid trouble.

The next day Traudl appeared on her daily walk with the baby and I gave her a nod of confirmation that our tryst was on the agenda. She smiled her acknowledgement. Now my nerves began to jangle. What had I committed myself to, and would I be brave enough to see it through? The enormity of the whole idea suddenly came into focus. I was going to risk my life for the possible reward of a kiss and a cuddle – if I managed to make the rendezvous and if Traudl turned up. My head was telling me I had lost my marbles and should stay in bed after lights out, but

39

my heart was shouting that I should give it a try. In this type of contest, I don't know of anyone who has listened to their head rather than their heart.

14

The weather could not have been better for my first attempt at breaking out of camp. It had been a beautiful sunny day with clear skies and good visibility. I had also checked that there would be no moonlight that night.

My nerves were jangling like a fire alarm bell and the strain on my innards was horrendous. I knew that I couldn't show the state I was in or Jimmy would never have agreed to my going out. So there I was, looking cool, calm and collected until it was time to go. After work we all made our way back to camp for a wash and change of clothes. Believe it or not, hygiene standards were extremely high; we had all learned that hygiene was easier than delousing. We all followed our normal routine. The evening meal was collected from the hotel, pleasurably eaten; then folowed the customary dish-washing and cleaning of the billet. After dinner everyone settled down to relating the adventures of the day or being bored to death listening to other people's stories, which of course we had heard time and time again.

At last the guard came to make the evening roll-call, which he did with his usual care and efficiency. Then we were safely locked in for the night, or so they thought. Timing was now critical. If the guard followed his normal routine, I had only ten minutes to clear the camp. Jimmy and Joe opened the trap-door in the kitchen while I was dressing, and with their best wishes ringing in my ears

I went down the hole and through to the outside toilet before I could even think of changing my mind. I replaced the toilet floor carefully, quickly checked the coast was clear and, without further ado, ran across the compound to the barbed-wire fence. In a couple of minutes I got through Joe's cleverly prepared hook-on gate at the bottom of the fence, and after carefully replacing it I reached the safety of the trees.

At this point I should have been able to relax and prepare myself for the next part of the outing. Instead I had to move like lightning and drop my trousers as all the years of constipation that I had suffered came to an abrupt end. I had literally scared the shit out of myself.

By the time I regained my composure, the problem of adjusting my eyes to the darkness was completely overcome. The visibility made me move with less caution than I should have to the safety of the woods on the other side of the road and onto the path leading to the village. It suddenly dawned on me that I might not be able to negotiate the few hundred yards to the spot where I hoped Traudl would be waiting for me. The path was almost invisible and my feet were warning me when I strayed onto rougher ground or it became too grassy. I walked with my arms outstretched and hands clasped together so that twigs and branches couldn't blind me if I got too near the trees. My ears were working overtime but fortunately on this first trip there was no wind to create any strange noises to jangle my already overstretched nerves.

Hidden animal instincts must have taken over and soon I was moving more freely and, more importantly, faster. In the excitement of solving the early problems, I had almost forgotten the object of the whole operation. With the adrenalin flowing, it all came flooding back and elation set in. There was a break in the trees where it seemed to be very light compared with the blackness of the woods. Suddenly I had reached the rendezvous point. Standing still and watching for Traudl was a tremendous relief – a bit like having climbed a mountain and enjoying the moment you have reached the peak. A new thought came to mind: even if Traudl didn't turn up, this would be a night to remember.

A slight movement to my left alerted me, and Traudl and I were re-united. There is no need to go into details of the next hour. I am sure everyone can remember his or her first big date. It can be awkward under normal circumstances, but here was I in a village under curfew, in enemy territory, trying to communicate in a foreign language of which I knew only a few words. We managed so well that we decided our next meeting should be indoors, since courting in the great outdoors at this altitude in winter was not on. Traudl showed me where her bedroom window was, at the back of the hotel, and conveniently on the ground floor. When we had a date in future, this window would be left unlatched and it wouldn't matter what time I arrived. Likewise, if anything went wrong and I didn't arrive at all it meant that Traudl would not be at risk wandering around at night after curfew. After a prolonged goodnight kiss, we decided time was up and I had to start back to camp and embark on the part of the night I hadn't thought about – breaking back into camp. Now I realised why the other blokes had stopped going out – the mere thought of getting back into camp was quite daunting, perhaps more hazardous than breaking out.

Making my way back through the woods seemed more difficult than before, and seemed to take twice as long. Once misgivings had set in, I almost lost the path. Everyone else was tucked up in a warm bed snoring away and here was I in the middle of the bloody woods wondering if I would reach the camp before dawn and praying that our guard was a sound sleeper. Fear spurred me on a bit faster and eventually I reached the edge of the woods. After a carefully reconnoitre of the camp area, I made my way to Joe's trap door in the perimeter fence. The camp lights all seemed to be spotlights focused on me, but I forced myself to move through the gap, carefully closing it behind me. A slow crawl followed to the toilet hut door, which I inched open and then crawled in. Frantically lifting the trap door, I moved quickly down into the tunnel and replaced the floor above me. Then I fainted. The relief of not having to concentrate on my movements had finally caught up with me. I could have quite happily gone to sleep in this little piece of no-man's land. When I came to, I completed the operation and very quietly undressed and slipped into my bunk. In no time I had passed into oblivion.

15

After the success of the first trip, the amorous outings became a regular routine. The only time they were curtailed in any way was due to weather conditions. When there was fresh snow on the ground after roll-call, it wasn't practical to risk making obvious tracks. After it had been well beaten down around the compound, however, I did go out in the snow. But when there was heavy cloud cover I also had to stay at home. One night I went out and everything went well until I entered the cover of the trees and it was totally dark – a blackness I had never experienced in my life before. It was like being inside a black velvet box inside a room with no windows or lights. After the first few yards of entering the woods I realised it would be impossible to go any further and when I turned round to go back I began to wonder how I was going to get out again. I had to resort to going down on my hands and knees and feeling for the path, then slowly inching forward until I was clear of the trees and the camp lights came into view.

Moonlit nights were also a problem as it could be too bright, and the combination of moonlight and snow made it impossible to go out. The best nights for travelling were the clear starlit nights with no wind, when visibility was fair and there were no strange noises to disturb my concentration. On such nights it was exhilarating to be on the move and clear of the camp and not to be a POW under constant surveillance.

It was on such a night that, having reached the shelter of the trees, I had the strangest feeling that something was wrong. I stopped, listening and watching for any movement, but everything seemed to be normal. The feeling persisted so I stepped off the path and squatted under a big fir tree and waited, breathing very gently. It didn't take long to spot the large man-sized shadow going along the path in the direction I should have been taking. My brain raced with possible explanations of this new development. The only solution was to wait a couple of minutes and turn back into camp. When I explained to Jimmy, Joe and Bill James what had transpired, we came to the conclusion that the guard had spotted me on one of my trips and, instead of doing a body-count in the barrack-room, had decided to follow and find out where I was going.

The guard in question at this particular time was a very

nice bloke. Tall, good-looking and softly spoken, he had told us that he would do any boot repairs we required as this was a hobby of his. In return we were to give him no hassle. In fact he was so pleasant to have around that when we heard his wife was coming to visit for a weekend, we had a whip-round of odds and ends from our Red Cross parcels so they could have a tasty couple of days. It was strange to see this strapping big soldier with tears in his eyes, and it was worth it to see the smile of thanks from his wife. This same guard asked me to treat a nasty boil on his wrist because if he had returned to his Depot for treatment the chances of his being returned to our camp were slim. So, for both our sakes, I took on the job. In about a week, after treating it with a strong-smelling ointment, I extracted the big root, leaving a large hole which healed up nicely in about another week.

Having said all that, I have no doubt that he would have had no hesitation in doing his duty and reporting us to his seniors had he found us breaking any of the rules. So it was agreed that there would be no more 'flying', as Bill called it, until further notice. It was during this time that it became clear what harm my love life had done to my nervous system.

Everything was fine for the first five nights that I stayed at home doing nothing but being bored. This should have had a good therapeutic effect on me but my hormones set up their own protest and almost killed me. We had turned in as usual after roll-call and I settled down to sleep after lights out, having spent a good healthy day in the beautiful mountain air. All went well until about two o'clock in the morning – the time I usually returned from visiting Traudl. Suddenly I was wide awake, but never in my life had I been so wide awake. The intense awareness of noises in the far distance was frightening and my whole body began to react to this super-sensitivity. Progressive palpitations followed and I felt that my heart was going to explode. Within seconds of waking I was in such a state that I felt that death could be the only conclusion of this attack.

But after reaching its peak, the attack slowly eased off and I lay in my bunk, drained both mentally and physically, and gradually slipped into a deep dreamless sleep. In the morning when Jimmy called me to get up, I told him what happened and asked him to report me sick as I felt totally incapable of work. However, after a day of complete rest, I recovered and almost forgot what I had been through. We discussed the possibility of restarting nocturnal outings but it was agreed that it was still too soon after the last incident, so I signalled this information to Traudl on her next walk through the village. To this she gave me an understanding nod and a disappointed pout.

Camp life went on as usual for another two humdrum weeks, and then, like a bolt out of the blue, in the middle of the night my eyes shot open and it happened all over again. This attack seemed worse than the first one. It followed the same pattern, leaving me totally wrung out and exhausted. The thought of these attacks recurring terrified me, and I felt from their severity that my body would eventually succumb. A side-effect was that I became afraid to go to sleep.

16

Luckily, the acquisition of the radio intervened and took my mind off my own problems. It was the summer of 1943 and rumours were flying about regarding the state of the war. Up here in the mountains it was hard to believe that there was a world war going on. The weather was great, and we had plenty of food and acceptable clothing, but we always had a thirst to know what was going on in the real world. We felt the radio would be the answer, and if we were to start using the tunnel again it might as well be for the benefit of the whole camp.

The team having been picked, we decided to go out on the first clear moonless night. Most of the team had never broken out of camp before, so you can imagine the state of their nerves. Those of us who had been out before had to calm them down and convince them it would be a doddle. Personally, I wasn't looking forward to it one little bit. I knew my own capabilities in the dark, but how would the first-timers take to the new environment? It was a gigantic gamble, considering six men had to get out of camp and get back in again in a very limited time. We had all played games against the clock before for fun but this time we were laying our lives on the line. Was the prize really worth it? At least Jimmy and Bill were in the party, the other three being in the strong-man class. They were needed to carry the radio back over the mountain; Bill and I couldn't be relied on for this because of our gammy legs.

The weather held, the break-out sequence went like silk, the whole team behaving as if this was a nightly occurrence; with no untoward incidents we arrived at the target ahead of time. The gasthaus had just closed and the guests had all merrily departed. Bill and I reconnoitred the building to find a point of entry, which turned out to be a toilet window which had not yet been closed. After making sure there was no one in, we quickly and silently entered, knowing that Jimmy and the others were posted outside and would warn us of any danger if it came along.

I had actually used this particular toilet on occasions and knew exactly where the room with the radio in it was. There was no-one in the passageway, so we moved on, and while Bill stood guard at the door with his right fist cocked, I rapidly disconnected the set. In a few seconds it was out the toilet window and into Busty's waiting arms.

The return trip to camp was made in a state of high jubilation, and the clear winter air at over two thousand feet lent wings to our weary legs. With everyone except Bill and myself taking turns at carrying our precious cargo, we made excellent time back to the camp. Speed was important in case the alarm was raised and our guard telephoned to check whether all his charges were safely tucked up in bed. In the end, we never heard the theft mentioned in the village and we were never under suspicion. After all, who would think that such an escapade was possible?

17

Our triumphant return was greeted with great wonderment from the rest of the boys. After we had showed off our prize, it was stowed away in the kitchen tunnel entrance until we decided on a permanent site for it. We all agreed it wasn't sensible to keep it on the premises. Next night after roll-call, when we were safely locked in, the place was buzzing with excitement as we unearthed our new-found source of information and prepared to connect it up to our power source. Within minutes we discovered what Rabbie Burns meant when he wrote, 'The best laid plans o' mice and men gang aft aglay'. We discovered to our horror that our mains was at a different voltage from that in the village where we had stolen the set. The next step was to see if the whole of Karlsbrunn was on the same voltage as the camp. After a couple of days of asking around, we discovered that one side of the village was also on this different voltage. All we had to do was find a working point for the radio on the other side of the main road from the camp.

After various other possibilities were discarded, I suggested the cellar of the hotel where Traudl lived, depending on the availability of a power supply to operate the set. The outside door to the cellar was never locked but the door from the hotel to the cellar was locked and bolted from the inside. It was finally agreed to check this out as a first possible location, and within a couple of days we found out that there was a really archaic system of wiring in the cellar. There were no conduits at all and the various lights were fed from two insulated wires which ran along the arched roof. Halfway along the passageway we found a little empty room which didn't appear to be in use, so we decided that if we dug a hole and boxed it we could put the radio safely in there and make a lid which could be filled with earth, making it virtually undetectable. The insulation on the corridor wires would have to be tapped and two temporary leads connected to the set and removed after use.

Finally, the big night came when we were to test the set. Along with Vic, an air force bloke masquerading as army, I had the privilege of doing the initial trial run. I'll never forget that night. We went through the tedious rigmarole of setting everything up, switched on and Vic tuned in to Victor Sylvester at the Hammersmith Palais. He was ecstatic; I had difficulty convincing him he couldn't listen to the end of the programme.

A listening rota was set up – two men going out together –
and so our BBC information service came into being.
For the first time, the real news of the war was available
to us.

18

It was around this time that we were told we would be
taking part in a historic piece of remodelling of the
Altvater mountain servicing. The electricity supply at
the mountain top was from an old-fashioned generator
and they wanted us to extend the supply cable from
Karlsbrunn to the top of the mountain, about another two
thousand feet. We were devastated and said that it would
be an impossible task for our small working party. To our
surprise, the authorities agreed and said they were going
to supplement our workforce with a dozen ditch-diggers
from the land of Oz.

The Aussies duly arrived and I have never seen such
a hand-picked bunch of mobile muscle before or since.
They were on a par with our own tame Aussie, Arthur. We
had been told that there would be no mechanical help
in the ditch-digging, but when we saw our new assistants,
the job became a possibility. The work distribution was
to be ten yards of ditch per day per man and everything
worked out well, except when we struck solid rock. Then
the dynamiter had to be called in.

Things didn't go too well with our new workmates, who
tried to take over the nice quiet running of our camp.
This led to continual resetting of Bill's knuckles as he
dealt with them one at a time. But, just as all good things
come to an end, so too did this bad job. Our gallant allies

were duly returned whence they came and the normal routine returned. This also meant that I could safely resume my love life with Traudl, which had ceased on the arrival of the Aussies as they were never told anything of our nocturnal activities. We also suffered a news blackout during this period.

19

The war news was turning very much in our favour now and the effect was beginning to show in a variety of ways. Any mention of the Eastern Front brought a look of terror to the face of any German. The war was going badly in Russia and troops returning home on leave were telling horror stories of conditions at the front. The enormous numbers of wounded returning home also told their own story.

Can you imagine the impact of the loss of 240,000 men in the Stalingrad area alone through fighting, hunger, cold and disease? It was now January 1943. There was still no significant breakthrough and talk of a second front in France was still only talk. The death-toll continued to rise on all fronts.

The flags and banners with their Swastika inserts seemed to hang rather limply now, the German chins seemed to droop a bit and the buoyancy that had been there a couple of years before was missing. We were not having to endure the full impact of war because places like Sudetenland and East Prussia lived fairly comfortably off their local produce and were not strategic targets for the Allied bombers.

The war had no effect on my love life and I was seeing Traudl about once or twice a week, though how she put up with my immature lovemaking I'll never know. The snowy winters provided a number of problems for us. Our arrangements for my entry to the hotel, through her unlatched bedroom window, worked fine in beautiful summer weather but it was not feasible after a fresh fall of snow; the local gossips would have had a field day. Traudl decided to provide me with a front door key as there was always a well trodden path to the door. We agreed that if fresh snow fell after lights out, my visit would automatically be cancelled.

Since I had started making these night visits, I had learned how to move quietly, and in situations where there was total darkness to feel with both my hands and feet as I moved. Even to this day I get shouted at for creeping up on people because I move so quietly.

Traudl came up with a brilliant idea during our first winter in Karlsbrunn. The snow at altitude is perfect for much of the time, and like most of the villagers Traudl had been brought up on skis. She and her younger brother were about the most daring skiers in the village. Sometimes I could hardly bear to watch their dangerous antics through the trees, but Traudl just laughed and said there was nothing to it. When I remonstrated with her to be more careful, she suggested that the way to cure my fear for her was to learn to ski myself.

Traudl said that there was an old pair of her father's skis in the attic and she had spare sticks which I could use, so all we had to do was arrange a suitable day and time for my first lesson. The guard knew I had been having bad headaches so he was quite amenable to my having a day off. During his time off, I left the camp and went to meet Traudl on the mountain. After about two hours' tuition from an accomplished skier like her I was able to do the basic snowplough and eventually a pretty poor Christiana. Other lessons followed when possible, and eventually I could herringbone up the slopes and ski down them.

The skiing era didn't last very long, because when some of the other lads miraculously acquired skis, it didn't take long for the guard to ferret out the hiding places of all the skis, which then disappeared forever.

20

Fate must have decided that we had had things too good for too long. Our nice guard was removed and replaced by two 'Wasser Polaks'. This happened about the beginning of 1944 and the new policy was a general tightening up as regards POWs. Their value was increasing as the German situation deteriorated. Apparently, if five or more prisoners escaped together, the matter had to be reported directly to the Führer. For us the holiday was over, and slowly a feeling of animosity crept in between the guards and ourselves.

This erupted violently one day. We were all returning to camp in the evening after work; as we entered the compound, the younger of the two guards decided to help matters along and pushed the prisoner in front of him through the gate. The unfortunate guard didn't know that there were two men in our camp you didn't push around, one being Bill James and the other Davey Jay. I don't know what Bill's reaction would have been but Davey's was instantaneous.

A quick shuffle of feet brought him round to face the guard, another fast adjustment to balance his body properly, then a lightning short right which hit the guard between the eyes with the full force of Davey's weight behind it. Another shuffle of feet brought Davey round again and he completed his entry into the barrack-room. Those of us who saw the incident were shocked at how quickly it happened and very smartly got into our compound, closing the gate behind us. We knew there would be an aftermath but none of us could have guessed just how horrible this would be.

Pandemonium reigned in our hut as word of what had happened went round the others. One of the lads watching at the window reported that the guard had crawled into his own hut. The calmest bloke in our hut was Davey, who sat on his bunk and tried to ignore all the fuss, though possibly he was going over in his mind the trouble that would arise from his uncontrolled action.

The waiting became intolerable. The guard who had been hit was trying to piece together what had happened when the other guard asked him if he had seen his damaged face, so he looked in the mirror. Right on cue we heard the screams of rage from the guards' hut. Within seconds, two very angry guards were in our hut and all hell broke loose. When we actually saw the damage that one punch from Davey had done we were shocked. Both the guard's eyes were rapidly discolouring and the bridge of his nose was swelling and taking on horrible rainbow hues. Somewhere he had lost his forage cap but in his right hand he had his unsheathed bayonet and his fellow guard had his rifle at the ready.

In a blind, mad rage the guard was swinging his bayonet in wide circles until finally he had Davey cornered alone. The other guard had the rest of us herded at the other end of the room and made it clear to us there was a bullet up the spout and the safety catch was off.

Davey was sitting on the edge of his bunk; the guard's vicious swing with the bayonet caught him unawares and hit him on the crown of the head. Blood spurted and we all shouted or screamed but the guard with the rifle again made his intentions quite clear. He would brook no interference in what was going on behind him. Davey saw the next blow coming and held up his hand to ward it off. The blade sliced down through his fingers, causing another surge of blood and more screams from us.

The sight of the blood must have helped to bring the guard back to his senses, and as suddenly as they stormed in they stormed out. First thing on the agenda was to tend to Davey's wounds as he was in a state of shock. Bill quickly decided that the Village Director should be notified and Busty was dispatched over the wire to attend to this. Davey required immediate hospitalisation, and God knows what the guards would get up to next. They might decide that, having gone this far, they might as well complete the job and wipe out the whole lot of us.

However, nothing further happened before the Director arrived. He promptly relieved the guards of duty pending their return to barracks and replaced them with temporary civil guards. He arranged transport to take Davey to hospital and then took a detailed report of the events. In one hour, our peaceful world had been turned upside down. The death knell had been sounded in our mountain Shangri-la, although we were lucky to have had two years of peace in this haven – especially when you think of the mass murder that was being committed all around us in the name of Christianity.

21

Traudl and I were naturally devastated by the turn of events, as it now became virtually impossible for me to carry on with my night visits to the hotel. Our romance would now be restricted to the odd loving glance if we saw each other in the village. To my mind this was a sad end to a remarkable piece of wooing but, on the credit side, it would give my badly shredded nerves a chance to recover.

It didn't take very long before we were informed that the working party would be wound up and all personnel returned to the main camp in Lamsdorf. This was extremely sad news after a happy two-year break in the Altvater mountains.

Many people might ask why no-one had escaped from such an easy camp, but it would have been extremely unfair to destroy a good situation like Karlsbrunn for those who had no wish to escape. The recommendation to anyone wanting to make a break from a good working party, of which there were very few, was that they return to the main camp and go out to a camp where another escape wouldn't do any harm.

Jimmy, Joe and I talked the whole thing over again and decided that we should now do something concrete about getting home, as it really looked like the war could go on for many years yet. In our present frame of mind we were ready to face the risks this entailed rather than sit tight in a worsening situation. The three of us, individually and collectively, began planning the complicated business of leaving Germany and returning home. I managed to steal a few minutes with Traudl in the cellar of the hotel one day and told her of our plans. She immediately insisted that we include her as there were many ways in which her help would be invaluable. For example, she could give us up-to-date information on the route we would be using, as travel restrictions changed continually due to bombing and troop movements. All three of us agreed that Traudl's plan made the most sense. After we returned to the main camp at Lamsdorf, we would arrange to come back to Sudetenland on a bad working party, escape from there and make our way back to Karlsbrunn, where Traudl would arrange to hide us while we made our final preparations for the journey home.

Everything began to move quickly now and only a week later we were back in Lamsdorf renewing our contacts with our Signals friends and all the others we had come to know in the past few years. It took about a week to tell them our adventures over the past two years and for them to bring us up to date on what had been happening in the main camp. We then got down to the business of finding out who the contact man was for the escape committee, and Jimmy and Joe arranged an appointment with them. The result of this meeting was completely negative. We were informed that no help could be given to first-time escapees. Jimmy got quite annoyed with me when I raged on about this stupid policy of having to prove that you were a loser before they would help you, instead of encouraging people who might get home on their first attempt. Why would anyone in their right mind keep giving assistance and material help to a constant loser who kept coming back like a rubber ball?

This meant that we were now out on our own, and any problems that arose would have to be solved by ourselves. I was still very optimistic about what lay ahead of us. The next step was finding a job back in Sudetenland and, soon enough, our chance came along.

Three replacements were required in a factory in the small town of Jagerndorf, which was about ten miles from Bad Karlsbrunn and suited our purposes admirably. So we volunteered for the job, and were accepted. We told our friends of our intentions; they wished us luck and a safe journey home. They also voiced their opinion that three was a crowd for such a venture. We reassured them that as a team we had survived so far.

A couple of days later the guard who was to accompany us to the job picked us up and we were off on our travels again. The pleasure on entering Sudetenland again was as great as the last time, and the three of us felt like children setting out on a great adventure, the first chapter of which would begin when we arrived at our new camp.

We were marched in through the standard wall of barbed wire, which of course would be no problem to Joe's educated pliers. However, when we came face to face with the concrete blockhouse with iron-barred windows and barbed wire on the outside, you could have knocked us down with the proverbial feather. When the guard handed us over and we were allocated our bunks, we were then locked in until mealtime. Inside were concrete walls, concrete floors and a concrete ceiling – and those damned iron bars looked more horrible from the inside than they had from the outside.

22

Being left alone inside this impregnable fortress was possibly the best thing that could have happened to us at this time. The three of us had all very different thoughts about the situation we were now in and had the opportunity to express our views in private. Jimmy was of the opinion that maybe we were being given the opportunity to call the whole thing off and, under the circumstances, I had to agree with him fully. Joe just couldn't believe that it could end with a whimper and not with a bang.

We agreed to discuss it with the camp leader and explain that we had come to this camp for the sole purpose of escaping and, if he had no objections to this, ask him if he had any ideas on how we might achieve a night escape from such formidable premises. This we did after having a meal and a natter with all the lads when they came in after work. His advice was to say nothing to anyone about the escape plans, with the exception of the two Glasgow men whom we had met with the others.

Over the years I have found that rather than rant at fate for being unkind at times, it is better to be a little philosophical and to count your blessings. It's amazing how often things come right in the end. Who would have believed that in the present circumstances there was any glimmer of hope that we would achieve our objective?

One of the Scots boys was called Danny and he almost ended himself with laughter when he heard that we had arrived in a strange camp on Friday and wanted to make our break on the Sunday night. He went on to explain that he and his friend had their escape planned for the coming June and that they had been setting it up for almost a year, so what was our hurry? We explained to him that four years had always been our target and that if we were prisoners as long as that, then we would have a go at getting home. Time was up.

Mentally we were prepared to have a go and the three of

us felt that any delay at this time would probably erode our plans and let us sink into a state of apathy. Thinking about escaping and actually doing it were two very different things, which accounted for the small number of escapees. After all, you were literally laying your life on the line when you broke out of camp and not many were prepared to do that.

Danny and his friend had a quick pow-wow and told us that if we were so desperate to go now, we were very welcome to use the facilities they had set up. We naturally remonstrated with them that this would be detrimental to their escape later but they insisted so heartily that I got the impression they were glad to get the idea of them having to go brought to an end. They then proceeded in great detail to explain that their preparations were complete and drew us diagrams of what they had done and how they had done it.

As we agreed, a daytime break was out of the question because you need time to get clear of the area before the manhunt starts, whereas if you start after roll-call at night, then you have until the next morning to get clear. The two boys had worked this out correctly and came up with the most astonishing method of overcoming the problem of getting out of the barrack-room. They knew that the roof, the walls and the floor were out of the question, so it had to be through the windows, which to their minds were the weakest part of the set-up. They went on to explain how they dealt with the vertical iron bars set in concrete, passing through lateral flat bars also set in concrete.

The upright bar, which had to be cut, was pencil-marked above and below the two lateral bars. A rope was then tied around the upper laterals and wound tight until the mark to be cut was exposed, then, with a very fine-bladed hacksaw, the bar was cut through. When the cut was completed, chewing gum was inserted in the space and the rope was removed, allowing the lateral bar to return to its normal position. This cut was repeated on the lower part of the bar and again chewing gum was inserted in the space and the lateral bar returned to its normal position. We were invited to have a go at finding out which bar was the one to be removed, and though the three of us tried our damnedest, we had to admit defeat.

When we asked Danny to show us which one it was, he laughed and said that when we were ready to go they would take the bar out and when we were gone they would put it back. This worried me a little, as I would have liked to see that it actually worked; timing was critical once we started our break. However, it would probably have taken us the best part of a year to get to where we could have managed on our own, and here was Danny handing it to us on a plate. Joe said that he had total trust in our new friends and Jimmy said that it would be all right on the night. And none of us even dreamed of asking where they got the hacksaw!

23

Our main objective now was to appear to be settling in to our new environment, and this we did thoroughly. In this we made a terrible, but simple, mistake, for which we were to suffer badly. Sunday was a day of rest for everyone, but as the football pitch was now clear of its winter coating of snow, the lads decided to have their first game of the season. When they found out that the three of us played, they were highly delighted as it gave them two full teams.

In view of what we had planned, you might think that at least one of three sane men would have realised that this was not a sensible thing to do, but we indulged ourselves in a full ninety minutes of our favourite sport. The old adage about living and learning is a lot of rubbish.

Since we had arrived in the new camp, I had checked the star formations at night and had lined them up in the direction that we had to take to hit Karlsbrunn. I was, of course, presupposing that we would have a clear sky on the big night. I had acquainted myself with our route on the local maps we had but, of course, there was the black-out to be taken into consideration, plus the curfew, plus the Home Guard, plus dogs in kennels and farms that could raise alarms, plus the unknown and the unexpected. It would have been so much easier to sit and wait until our gallant troops came to relieve us – but, as I said, hormones don't listen.

That Sunday night we did our final checking and planning, and on Monday morning we went off and did a normal day's work. We were never inside the factory; it was said to be a parachute production outfit, though we couldn't verify this in any way because of the high-security conditions surrounding the area. Anyway, we were not going to be there long enough to find out.

The weather was at its very best, with a clear sky and a light spring breeze; if it lasted through the night, it would be perfect for our trip. I knew there would be no moon that night and it looked as if there would be no cloud cover either. At least the elements were working in our favour.

Finally, our working day was over and we were feeling no ill-effects from the football, so we returned to the camp in good spirits. We began to make the final preparations after our evening meal in order to be ready to go after roll-call, leaving no signs behind that we had ever been there at all. Danny and the others still had their doubts that we would really make the break, but we finally convinced them that we were leaving and that we would send them a postcard when we got home.

Jimmy, Joe and I had a final huddle to make sure that there were no last-minute second thoughts, as the effort had to be one hundred per cent, and the three of us confirmed that it was all systems go. Danny and his mate had the equipment they required to release the bar in the window, and we had the clothes we were to travel in safely out of sight. Our order of dress was normal underwear and shirt, boots and socks, dark trousers and a heavy dark pullover. Other than this, we would each carry a light snack to be consumed on the march. In addition Jimmy would have a first-aid kit, Joe would have his pliers and I would have my maps and a small battery torch I had acquired. The reason that we were travelling so light was that this first part of the break had to be successful. If it failed, then would come the time for improvisation.

24

Roll-call. The next half-hour could possibly be the most exciting time of our lives, or – with bad luck – it could be the end of our lives. This was always the alternative when you left camp without permission, and I knew the horrible feeling I had had in the pit of my stomach every time I had gone to see Traudl. I also knew that Jimmy and Joe must be going through hell at the thought of what was in front of them. Fortunately, they showed nothing of this while the guards went through their dreary routine of counting their flock for the last time that day. I can vouch for it that, on this occasion, everyone was present and correct.

Finally satisfied, the guards withdrew; as soon as the key clicked in the lock, Danny's team attacked the window that we were to go through. We three began to change into the clothes we were going to leave in. Time was now of the essence, as we knew that in about fifteen minutes the first perimeter patrol would begin and before that we would have to be completely clear of the camp.

All three of us hit the finishing tape together in our personal preparations and Danny signalled that the window was cleared for Joe to operate on the barbed wire on the outside – which he promptly did. Danny had told us that when we hit the ground on the outside we should get going immediately, and he would close up the wire and restore everything to normal. This was an amazing blessing with time so short. Jimmy was to go first as he was the biggest; if he got out safely, then our first problem was solved. He had worked out how he would make the difficult exit through the space in the bars. Joe and I watched him very carefully. In a few seconds he was out and dropped to the ground. Joe followed, and I was right behind him.

With a quick 'thumbs up' to the boys watching at the window, we were off and running to the part of the perimeter fence that we had decided to go through. In about half a minute, Joe had cut enough barbed wire to let us crawl through, and half a minute later he had it resealed. This done, we stole away to the cover of some trees nearby. As soon as we were in cover, we silently hugged each other in congratulation, and then it became my problem to take the lead and guide us to the promised land which, in this instance, was Bad Karlsbrunn.

Away from the lights of the compound, the darkness became more intense, but our eyes rapidly adjusted and it was a beautiful clear starlit night – better visibility than many of the nights that I had already been out. The adrenalin was still running high, and we had to put as much distance as possible between ourselves and the camp. It took about five minutes before I picked up the road that would take us out of town and finally on to Karlsbrunn. Twenty minutes later we were almost clear of the last houses and reaching the open countryside. Our plan was to use the main road as much as possible, as this was the only way we could cover the distance involved and reach our destination before dawn. We removed the heavy socks that we had pulled over our boots when we were moving through the area with houses and would put them on again when we felt we were too loud. They would have worn through too quickly if we had kept them on all the time.

We kept silent while we were marching but stopped at odd intervals for a confab. We even had to stifle our giggles on the first rest when we all agreed that our eyes and ears felt ten times as big as normal.

Our first problem came when we approached a village right on the main road. How were we going to deal with it? The choice was either to walk straight through or go round it. For safety's sake we decided to take the long route. In daylight it might have been a simple detour, but at night we lost so much valuable time and got into such a mess that we decided to take the direct route in future. It began to dawn on us that at our present rate of progress we were not going to reach our target on time, so we agreed to step up the pace. This is when we discovered what our stupid game of football had done to us. Within an hour of going at the faster speed all three of us were feeling the effect on our leg muscles, and as we were almost continually climbing now, the strain was getting worse all the time. We knew that we had to be under cover before daybreak; the alarm would be raised by then, and to be out in the open would be fatal. I had no idea where we might hide safely for a whole day in the woods.

By my reckoning we still had about ten kilometres to go and dawn was only a couple of hours away. Normally this would have been no great problem, but with our leg muscles screaming for rest, it was becoming cripplingly clear that the odds were against us arriving on time. We stopped for a couple of precious minutes and talked over the situation. We decided it was a case of heads down and try our damnedest. Maybe the pains would go away. They didn't, but they didn't get any worse, and I think what saved us was that none of us wanted to be the one to say that he couldn't go on.

There were no more villages to go through, so it was a straight slog all the way now. The miles slowly rolled by and, in these final stages, I think our brains became numb, although I can't say the same for our legs, which continued to complain bitterly about their treatment. The sky was becoming noticeably lighter when we reached the top of our climb, and this was where we had to part company; Jimmy and Joe were to make their way to a hut in the forest which was once used by hunters. We had discovered it when we worked in Karlsbrunn and had stowed away a couple of blankets there, which would be very useful for the boys. I now had to make my way down behind the village to Traudl's hotel and see if it was safe to climb in the bedroom window which, God and Traudl willing, I might find unlocked.

We said our 'auf wiedersehens' and arranged our contact times. We parted company, hoping that all would go well for both parties.

25

Jimmy and Joe were to keep under cover in the hut while I tried to forge some kind of travel documents for us. Without these it would be impossible to travel by train. From what we had learned over the last four years, rail was the only way we could possibly cover the distance from Sudetenland to the northern coast at Stettin. From Stettin we would try to stow away on a ship going to Sweden. To do a good job of the travel documents I would, of course, have to have warm comfortable surroundings and a source of the necessary materials. Traudl's bedroom was the obvious place, and the source was to be Traudl herself. How lucky can you get?

When I parted from the boys, I worked my way down to the rear of the hotel via the trees on the upper side of the village, and by this time it was almost daylight. After a quick look around to check that the coast was clear, and a smart walk with my heart in my mouth, I was directly under Traudl's window. With a prayer on my lips I jumped for the ledge below the window and pushed up the lower part of the window. It opened smoothly.

Seconds later, I was over the sill and safely into my favourite bedroom. Once inside, I watched intently for a while to see if there was any movement in the vicinity, but everything remained peaceful. The night-light at the bedside came on and Traudl was holding out her welcoming arms. In no time at all I was snuggled down and felt as if I would never get out of bed again. The euphoria didn't last long; Traudl whispered that it was time for her to go on duty and that when she left the room I would have to lock the door from the inside so that on-one could enter, even with a pass key.

This led to a very frightening experience for the poor girl, as it was twelve hours later before I heard her knocking to get in. When I opened the door she was in a terrible state; she had tried to wake me at various times during the day without success, and only at six o'clock in the evening did she succeed, finally delivering the meal that she had lovingly prepared earlier.

As she was now off duty, we had a long talk about all that had happened since we last met. Then we discussed what was to be done about the documents we needed. Traudl thought that the simplest solution would be for us to carry the normal German identity cards; when she showed me hers, I agreed that to copy them might just be a possibility, given that we could obtain materials to do the job. And so to bed.

Next day I began the search for paper as close as possible in texture and colour to the ID card that had to be copied. I finally found blank pages in some old books that would do nicely. Traudl produced a variety of pens and different inks because, apart from the print, there were also rubber stamps to be copied. Only when we had all the materials together did it finally dawn on me that the most important thing for an ID card was missing – our photographs. I nearly cried.

Traudl wisely pointed out that passport and ID photos were never really a close likeness anyway. She then produced all the photographs of men from the family albums that were approximately the right size. Not one

of the photos looked like any of us three. We made a
choice of three, on the most tenuous of grounds. One
appeared to be blond, so that would be Jimmy. Of the
other two, one couldn't possibly be Joe so he would have
to be me. That left one, who must be Joe. In the end, it
was all very simple.

I spend four tense and tiring hours working on the first
ID card copy, but when I stopped and really looked at
it, the result was so poor that it got torn up and thrown
in the fire. Instead of feeling despondent about my first
attempt, I buckled down to the fact that I would have
to do better and in the next two days produced what I
thought were a couple of masterpieces. Traudl agreed
that they were not bad and came up with the brilliant idea
of acquiring three plastic holders for them, which would
help to disguise them a bit. At a quick glance, folded with
the photo and identity particulars outward inside the
holders, they looked quite authentic, we thought. Next
day I finished the two pages that would be exposed on the
third ID and decided not to bother with the eagle, swastika
and other details on the inside as they wouldn't be seen.
Thus I completed the third and final document.

At least that's what I thought. When the boys and I made
our rendezvous in the woods that night and I explained to
them what I had done, they were both adamant that the
third card should be completed and it didn't matter how
tired or fed up I was. So I had to go back to the drawing
board. Their insistence on the completion of the third
card saved our lives later, as it turned out. Next day, I
grudgingly finished the job. We were now at the stage
where we must move on, as we had endangered Traudl
for far too long.

26

Our next step was to collect the escape clothing that we had hidden away in Karlsbrunn previously, including the iron rations we would be carrying to help us reach our destination. These consisted mainly of chocolate and biscuits and a few tins of meat, all of which had been saved from our Red Cross parcels. Also included in this valuable hoard was the German currency that we had acquired from various sources. This was added to the money we had accumulated on our last visit to the main camp. Two old briefcases and an old rucksack completed our new civilian outfits, as all of the workmen carried these, or something similar, when they were on the move. Our shaving gear, plus a towel, soap and comb, had come with us from Jagerndorf and would naturally be included.

Traudl had been working hard to teach me the most likely phrases that might be required on the journey, such as buying train tickets or asking directions, or things you might want to ask in a restaurant. Her advice was that the best person to ask was a policeman. This made good sense to me as they have local knowledge. At home they're the most helpful of people and Traudl said they were the same in Germany.

We had been a bit concerned about the weather; there had been a slight flurry of snow on the day that we decided our preparations were complete. However, it cleared quite quickly and the spring sun shone again, so we made up our minds to get on with it. The decision made, we were off next day, at the ungodly hour of 2 a.m.

This part of the journey required us to go on foot from Karlsbrunn, mainly downhill, some eight or nine miles to the railhead at Wurbenthal, the same station we had arrived at two years before when we came from upper Silesia, and also on our return to Sudetenland fairly recently. There was a local bus which made this run but, after working in the area for two years, we couldn't take the chance of someone recognising us.

Traudl and I said our final farewells, and after a tearful parting and a promise to return, I left to join the boys and continue our journey home. Since we had broken out of camp in Jagerndorf I don't think I ever entertained one negative thought about being recaptured. Even though we still had over two hundred and fifty miles to cover as the crow flies, I felt it was a one-way journey. It is just as well that we didn't know that fate was setting up one of the biggest booby-traps in history.

At two o'clock on the morning of 25 March we set off at a leisurely pace, knowing that on this stage there was no urgency. We had lots of time to reach the station and catch our train. March in the mountains could be very chancy for weather, but today there was a real touch of spring in the air, which transferred itself to our legs. We all felt fit after our enforced rest, but there was a touch of sadness at finally leaving Karlsbrunn, which had sheltered us from the horrors of war for two peaceful years.

The road we were now taking was reputedly traffic-free at night, and tonight was no exception. We knew there was only one small village to pass and our rapid downhill progress needed to be slowed down drastically. Our arrival at Wurbenthal had to coincide with the early morning movements of the local population. An old barn at the roadside provided us with the ideal shelter for an hour's rest. Joe had to move from the original heap of straw that he sat on when it began to move, but he apologised politely and found another unoccupied spot with no nest of mice. Once we set off, the aim was not to be furtive, but at all costs to avoid being conspicuous. When we finally entered the town, there was enough early morning movement to keep us comfortable as we made our way to the railway station.

I wonder if you can imagine how I felt when I had to approach that little window and ask for three tickets to Sagan. It would either be the beginning or the end of our journey. What would happen? Stagefright maybe, with no words coming out. Total loss of memory of the German phrases I had so painstakingly learned? Maybe Jimmy or Joe wouldn't mind going over and buying the tickets. It was the bren-gun situation at La Capelle all over again. Why couldn't I keep my mouth shut instead of saying: 'All right, I'll do that!'?

When the dreaded moment came, I detached myself completely and watched from outside as my body went to the window, asked for the tickets, paid for them and received the change, then turned and walked away almost jauntily. Jimmy and Joe congratulated me on my cool behaviour, but I didn't tell them how it had been done.

27

I thought that the most difficult part of the journey was over. The problem of buying the tickets had been giving me nightmares ever since I had been elected to do it. I had thought that three fit young men in civilian clothes would stick out like a sore thumb, when we should have been wearing a uniform of some kind – any kind. I can only imagine that we had spent so much time in France that perhaps we had picked up a slightly French aura. As the Laval scheme, which used French civilian workers, was in full swing, maybe we were mistaken for French.

Our train was due to leave in about five minutes, and a fair number of people were hanging about waiting to board, so we just followed the general trend of looking tired and fed up. Soon we were seated uncomfortably on the hard benches in the quietest part of the coach we could find. Following almost everyone else's example, we leaned back and closed our eyes as the train slowly and noisily left the station. It turned out to be one of those trains we had heard about – the kind you could get off to pick flowers while it's in motion and rejoin. It also seemed to stop at the least excuse and very often for no reason at all. But it was better than walking and there would be faster sections on the way north, we hoped. Otherwise, it seemed, we were doomed to spend the rest of our lives on this train.

Sagan surprised us at about midday, and quite a few passengers got off with us. We found ourselves walking stiffly, like John Wayne. Maybe he travelled a lot on the old trains with wooden seats. It certainly knocks hell out of your circulation.

If our intelligence information turned out to be correct, then there was a fairly large French civilian camp just outside the town, and this was our first target; we wanted to find out if their hospitality was really as good as we had been led to believe. Under no circumstances would we ever approach any Poles for help; all the escapees who had done so seemed to end up back in camp – though there must have been exceptions to this.

There seemed to be an inordinate number of people standing about but it could have been in aid of some sort of celebration or special market day. We shrugged off any thoughts we had about this and went on our way to find our French friends. How do you find a Frenchman in a country full of Germans? Our time in France must have helped us, because within minutes we spotted two blokes who just had to be what we were looking for. When we got closer and could hear them talking, we knew that we had hit the jackpot. We asked them to take us to their leader – or words to that effect – and, with the few French words that we knew added, they got the message and pointed out to us the man we were looking for in a shop across the road.

When he came out, we crossed over to introduce ourselves, but when we explained to him that we were three Scottish soldiers on the run from a prisoner-of-war camp, the poor man went very pale and almost wobbled at the knees. Thinking that maybe he had heard some strange stories about the Scots, we told him that we were only looking for some temporary shelter and perhaps a bite to eat. He was slowly regaining his natural sallow colouring and, having got over the shock of hearing who we were, told us in good and fluent English to please leave his presence at once as he did not wish to be seen speaking to us. This was not what we expected to hear from a gallant ally. As he started to move away, we more or less surrounded him and asked what his problem was; had we said something to offend him?

Realising that we wanted an answer, he quickly explained that a mass escape had taken place the previous day from the local RAF camp, namely Stalag Luft Drei, and that it could only be minutes before we were questioned and arrested. Now it was our turn to go pale. With a short apology for not being able to help us, the camp leader smartly disappeared. We looked at each other in stunned silence, and slowly a picture formed in my mind of all the strange-looking people we had seen in the railway station when we arrived. They began to take shape as members of the Gestapo, the German CID, and many other punitive organisations. They were all looking for escaped POWs – not us, necessarily, but that would make no difference. Short of carrying a placard stating that we had escaped from Sudetenland and not from the RAF camp, there was no way out of this dilemma.

Our brains began to function again, and without a word being said, we slowly walked away from the station till we reached a nice quiet spot where we could talk safely. We agreed that we were in it right up to our necks and that there couldn't possibly be a way out; the whole area must be alive with forces with just one thought in mind.

Joe suggested that we head out into the open country and try to work our way north. I pointed out that we had made no provision for travelling in this manner and it would be far too slow. Apart from that, it would be very difficult to find places to stop for the night before curfew. Also, not having a detailed map of the whole area between here and Stettin made it virtually impossible. Jimmy quietly asked what I had in mind. When I told them, they both looked at me in astonishment, then all three of us burst into hilarious laughter at such a frighteningly stupid idea. My proposition was that we return to the station and carry on with our original plan of moving on to Frankfurt after our stop at Sagan.

The tall, lean French camp leader might have exaggerated the whole business and his idea of a mass escape might have been five or six airmen – in which case there was probably no need for our present panic. The only way to verify this was to return to the station. We kicked the idea around for a few minutes and came up with a unanimous decision to take the easy way out. As soon as we re-entered the station, we knew that the bloke had not exaggerated. Practically all the men in the station were being stopped and asked to produce their papers by a variety of stern-faced teams of two and three. I remembered something that Traudl had told me about coupon-free soup and, after we established that our train didn't leave for another forty minutes, we headed in the direction of the station restaurant and ordered three plates of the same. The waiter scowled at us in a most unfriendly manner, but I suppose it could have been because he had had a row with his wife or, even worse, his girlfriend. Half an hour soon passed and we prepared to leave. Just as we were going through the door, Jimmy turned round and, to our amazement, stared right at the waiter and rapped out a loud 'Heil Hitler'. The waiter reacted as if he had been shot but came smartly to attention and answered Jimmy's greeting. Outside we asked Jimmy why he had done it. He admitted that it had been totally spontaneous but he did feel that the waiter needed smartening up a bit and it would certainly remove any suspicion from his mind.

In fear and trepidation I now went to buy our tickets to Frankfurt. After paying for them I checked which platform we departed from. With the skin on my back crawling with fear, we headed for the platform, feeling we were never going to make it. Five minutes later the train pulled out; we hadn't been stopped. I could hardly believe our luck. We were not invisible, because I could still see Jimmy and Joe as large as life. We had sprung the booby trap and come out unscathed. Our problem now was to reach Frankfurt in time to find help before curfew. Would you believe it, the first thing we heard on our arrival at Frankfurt was the happy chattering of four Frenchmen, almost as if they had been waiting for us.

It took a few minutes to convince them of who we were. Retaining their happy mood, they escorted us to their camp, which was not very far away. The camp leader was a real charmer who spoke some English; he made a very thorough job of interrogating us. When he was satisfied, he agreed we could stay for one night – which was all we wanted. Then they generously gave us something to eat and turned down our offer of a couple of bars of chocolate in return, saying that we would probably need them before our journey was over. Conversation proved to be difficult so, when we were shown where to bunk down for the night, we gladly got our heads down. It took quite a while to stop our minds turning over the events of the day time and again. Exhaustion eventually won and a dreamless sleep ensued.

28

All three of us woke next morning feeling fully recuperated and happily able to talk freely in English which, of course, we were unable to do most of the day. Fortunately, we had been living and working together so long that quite often a look or an inclination of the head could convey the message. Our telepathy was put strenuously to the test during our trip, but worked wonderfully well.

Over a cup of ersatz coffee and a roll, we went through the events of the previous day. None of us could come up with a plausible explanation of what had transpired in Sagan station. We had seen the Controls stopping people and checking their documents. Joe had also spotted the French camp leader in the station, no doubt waiting to see us being arrested. He too was probably left wondering why we hadn't been stopped.

Anyway, the next step was to wash and shave in comfort. After having thanked the camp leader for his hospitality, and accepted his kind offer of a guide to take us back to the railway station, we gave him a big Gallic hug. Then we moved back into the real harsh world outside, wondering what Fate had in store for us on this bright sunny day. We had decided to book all the way from Frankfurt to Stettin, not stopping at Angermunde as we had originally planned.

The train we were to catch was listed as an express; we had no illusions about what this meant, as we had been warned about long delays and possible diversions due to bombing raids. But suppose we were caught in a town which had just been bombed, where they were still digging out the dead and dying; what would happen to us? In our imaginations we thought we would be torn to pieces. This threat hung over every escapee. The moment you donned civilian clothes, you gave up the right to be treated as a POW and could quite correctly be prosecuted for espionage, which could carry the death penalty. If you were daft enough to escape and travel in your own national uniform, however, you would be safe if recaptured, as you would merely be returned to camp and punished.

Our biggest worry now was whether we would reach Stettin in time to make contact with our indispensable French allies before curfew time. The train left on time, so at least we were off to a good start, but we had only been travelling for about fifteen minutes when a heart-stopping incident occurred. The compartment was fairly full, with one small boy restlessly wandering up and down the aisle between the seats. After passing by several times he suddenly approached his mother, and pointing to us, told her that we were 'Englanders'. The three of us heard him quite clearly, and I'm sure that everyone could see the colour draining from our faces. I closed my eyes and waited for the inevitable to happen. Mummy quietly asked her son what gave him such a strange idea and his reply was that he could smell chocolate when he passed us. His mother gave an apologetic smile in our direction and told him to sit still and stop wandering about. They got off at the next stop.

We had failed to anticipate this method of being detected, but the remainder of the chocolate was wrapped more carefully, so that the smell didn't alert anybody else deprived of the taste. All the experience and knowledge we had accumulated in the past four years could have been nullified by a small boy who knew that the Englanders received chocolate in their Red Cross parcels. Someone probably told him this when they were explaining to him why he couldn't have any.

I glanced at Jimmy and Joe, who looked relaxed, yet my nerves felt completely shredded. I remember at one stage even thinking that if we were caught we could at least finally return to a normal way of living as POWs. Looking back on my nervous attacks in Karlsbrunn, which were still occurring but thankfully at longer intervals, I realised this trip could lead to a complete nervous breakdown. On the positive side, though, I was drawing strength from Jimmy and Joe all the time.

The landscape in this part of Germany was dull and boring, and we couldn't converse in English, so I spent most of the time with my eyes closed. Again and again my mind went back to Sagan station and the riddle of why we hadn't been stopped for a document check. The hypnotic rumble of the train finally helped me to come up with a possible solution. Supposing there had been someone in overall control of the checking operation and, again, supposing this person had seen us arriving on the train from the Breslau direction, then it would be noted that we were coming into Sagan and not trying to get out. Later, when we were leaving, this very efficient person remembered us and signalled that we were OK and not to waste time on us. Either that, or we had the luck of the devil.

I came back to reality with a bump as the brakes began to squeal in pain and we started the slow entry into Angermunde. The three of us exchanged smiles as this was the penultimate stop before Stettin. But we should have known better than to tempt Fate. Lined up on the platform was a group of German soldiers wearing 'Kontrolle' shields round their necks. When our train stopped, they spread out and began to enter the different carriages. Jimmy quickly leaned forward and whispered that there were to be no heroics, and if anyone of us was caught, then all three of us would go quietly. We nodded and sat back to wait for the inevitable to happen.

29

It was only now that I thought what a stupid waste of time the making of the identity cards had been. Although they had given us a sense of security, we never thought that if anyone seriously looked at them they could believe they were genuine. I remember feeling the whole thing was finally over, but we had acquitted ourselves well and at least the Escape Committee would have to take us seriously now. If they had helped us instead of the losers, the documents they would have provided might have seen us through this check. The little guard was slowly working his way towards us. He looked to be in his forties and was probably not physically fit enough to fight and die on the Eastern Front, but here he was about to recapture three British prisoners, for which he would probably be awarded the Iron Cross.

Finally, it was our turn and Jimmy cleverly fumbled a bit before producing his cellophane folder with his ID card in it. When I saw the uninterested look on the guard's face, I just couldn't believe it. He handed the card back and held out his hand for mine – a cursory glance later, it was returned. Joe was next, but here the pattern changed. In my head I was screaming that two out of three wasn't bad, but it looked now as if our luck was running out. The guard looked at Joe's card as he had looked at ours, but something about it seemed to disturb him. To satisfy himself he removed it from its folder, opened it up and examined the inside. When he saw the eagle and swastika insignia, he replaced it in the folder and handed it back without comment. He then moved on to the next seat. Was this the card that I hadn't wanted to finish? What made the guard want to check this one? Did he want to check to see if I had finished it?

The three of us sat in stunned silence, but it wasn't over yet. When the guard had finished his compartment check, the train started to move again and he came along and sat in the free seat next to Jimmy. We were so cocky that we had been mentally congratulating ourselves until this happened. Of course this clever little man had us spotted, and when the train stopped again we would be placed under arrest. And I had been thinking how stupid he was not to have seen that our documents were fakes!

We suffered silent torture for about another three miles and then the train began screeching, slowed down and stopped. The guard stood up and slung his rifle strap over his shoulder. This seemed to me to be a bit casual for an arresting officer as he should, of course, have had it at the ready in case there was any trouble. He didn't know that we wouldn't cause trouble. In fact, I was all ready to stand up and follow him at a nod of his head. But he slowly made his way to the door at the end of the compartment, opened it and left us without even a farewell.

When the train moved on, we looked at each other in total disbelief. We could see the guards who had been on the checking party assembling on the platform outside. I began to wonder if parts of this journey were real or just dreams that occurred when I dozed off. The compartment was almost empty at this time and the boys confirmed that I wasn't having nightmares. They had also thought that the guard had spotted us and had us under surveillance. More passengers came into our compartment at the next stop, which put an end to conversation, so we went back to our mental and physical relaxation positions in the hope of undoing the nervous damage we had suffered.

The feeling of tension was just beginning to wear off as we pulled into a small station near the end of our journey. Suddenly, a small girl on the other side of our compartment screamed 'Englanders!' My hands almost involuntarily shot up in the air, but then I saw Jimmy standing up and pointing to a working party of British POWs walking along the platform outside. As everyone was looking in the same direction, they didn't see the shocked look on our faces. First, the little boy with the highly developed nostrils, and now a sweet little girl with a shrill voice . . . We considered ourselves extremely lucky that the adults in Germany were not as perceptive as their children.

Our so-called express continued to inch its way slowly along and finally arrived in Stettin. The only indication we had that our destination had been reached was the fact that the train stopped and everyone got off. When we stepped onto the platform, there was no sign of a railway station as such, just rubble, which until very recently had been the station. There was a small wooden hut on the platform, which was obviously for the use of the railway staff, but the rest was desolation. We quickly agreed that we didn't want to be captured in this town so soon after a devastating bombing raid. As we walked slowly into the city centre, the damage became more apparent, but then we came upon one of the freaks of such raids. Right in the middle of the town stood a beautiful big red building, completely untouched, like a monument in the desert. As we passed it, we discovered that the building with the charmed life was the Head Post Office.

All three of us were now on the alert for the sight or sound of some Frenchmen.

30

A deep feeling of despondency seemed to affect the German people now. The war news from all fronts was bad and the number of wounded returning to the Fatherland was continually on the increase, especially from the Russian front, where the German troops were being mowed down by the thousand as they retreated. What with all this and the continual increase in the Allied bombing raids, it was becoming more evident that there could only be one outcome to the war. The Wonder Weapon had not materialised.

The Allies can only thank God and Werner von Braun and his team that they deliberately delayed their production of the first complete atomic bomb, otherwise there would probably, nay certainly, have been a different outcome to the war. However, with only conventional weapons, Hitler now had no hope of any kind of victory on land, sea or air. You would think that one look at a world atlas would have shown him the futility of trying to fight on so many fronts. On the other hand, he must have felt complacent about the way his troops swept through Poland and then pushed the British out of France (despite General Tiger Gort putting me in the front line as the final deterrent), and about the way his troops controlled the North African theatre of war for a period. Together with the toll that the U-boats took on our shipping, this must have convinced him and Germany that he could conquer the world. The euphoria of all the early successes had long since died. Now the reality of the mammoth task had become apparent, and the inevitable failure had to be faced – but could not be talked about, as this was forbidden. Hitler's pledge of total war had also been a dreadful mistake for the German people, as it left no loophole for a settlement, and could only end in unconditional surrender.

These thoughts ran through our minds as we walked through the town and absorbed the dismal mood of the people who, at the beginning of the war, would have raced from one street to another, just to get a glimpse of either Hitler or Göring. This enthusiasm didn't extend to Heinrich Himmler, however, as he preferred the streets empty and well guarded when he paid a visit to a strange town.

Soon these thoughts were interrupted by a very welcome sound: voluble French. We shadowed the two Frenchmen until they reached a convenient spot for us to approach them, then tried to make them understand who we were and what we needed. In the beginning there was the usual distrust, but then they felt our desperate need and finally agreed to take us to their camp, where their leader would make the final decision whether to help us or not.

This leader turned out to be a very charming man, and between his broken English and our almost non-existent French, we convinced him that we were genuine. He congratulated us on having come so far safely, and said that they would give us their wholehearted support and assistance. He pointed out that the toughest part of our journey was in front of us; he had never heard of anyone succeeding in breaking through the security cordon surrounding the port.

We were shown where we could have a bath, given a meal, and then shown where we could bunk down and have a good sleep in perfect safety. Next day, he told us, he would send someone with us to the dock area and we could make our first reconnaissance. From then on it would be entirely in Jimmy's hands. He had said all along that if we could get him to a seaport, he would get us out of it and home. So all he had to do was keep his promise.

When we saw the dock area next day, I began to have grave doubts. The actual shipping area could only be reached by crossing a bridge which, of course, was permanently manned by soldiers, and a special pass had to be shown by anyone wanting access to the docks. The boys suggested that we could swim over the river at some point, but not being a very strong swimmer, this didn't appeal to me one little bit. Jimmy decided that this was not an insurmountable obstacle and that first he had to find a seaman from a Swedish ship and find out when it would sail; then we could tackle the problem of getting into the docks.

That evening Joe and I were confined to quarters and Jimmy went off on his own. This was one of the few times during the war that we were separated, and Joe and I felt most unhappy about it, but Jimmy insisted that he had to do this on his own as it was safer. We could only sit, worry and wait, wondering if he would ever come back.

Three hours later we got the answer. Jimmy breezed in looking as if Scotland had won the World Cup, so we guessed that his mission had been successful. Sure enough, everything had turned out exactly as he had hoped, and as he regaled with us the details of his evening out, we realised that the final stages of our ambitious trip had become a possibility.

31

Jimmy explained to us that when he went into town he had to find the club, pub or brothel that the seamen on shore-leave used, so his target area would be near the docks. When he got down near the harbour, he met what looked and sounded like a bunch of sailors having a good time. Reckoning that they must be coming from the place he was looking for, he moved on in the direction they had come from. Sure enough, there it was, in the middle of the next block, looking just as it looked in ports all over the world.

He went in and ordered a beer, but when the pretty brunette barmaid starting asking questions, he excused himself and sat at a nearby empty table. Luck took a hand when five minutes later the door opened and a blonde bloke of about thirty came in. After ordering a beer at the bar, he looked around and saw Jimmy, who was about his age and also blonde, sitting alone and perhaps of the same nationality. He came across and indicated a wish to join him. With a nod of assent and a wave to the vacant seat next to him, Jimmy couldn't believe his luck: if anyone was watching him, they would see that he hadn't made the first approach. The stranger introduced himself. He was a Swede from a ship in the harbour and spoke a fair bit of English.

Without getting involved in a lot of lies or fairy stories, Jimmy decided to go for broke and told the Swede who and what he was, tentatively asking if there was any possibility of his new friend helping him to stowaway on his ship when it sailed. He was amazed at the reaction to this request. The man's face broke into a happy smile and he said that he would be delighted to take Jimmy back on board with him immediately, as his ship sailed with the tide in the early morning. He also said they would have no trouble entering the docks because if one of them had a shore-leave pass, the guard would assume they both had passes.

Now Jimmy had to explain there were three of us. Then, of course, the deal was off. Under no circumstances would the Swede contemplate taking three men into the docks. His offer to Jimmy still stood, but only if he came alone. After explaining that he couldn't do this, he asked if it was possible to give him the berth number the ship was lying at. This information was given grudgingly, but he did allow Jimmy to walk to the entrance to the docks with him, where, with a vague wave of his pass, he went through the control point. This was when Jimmy realised how we were going to get into the dock area by ourselves.

Having told us his story, Jimmy now told us to get ready to move and to dump all our kit except the clothes we were wearing; this was the last step in our bid to get home. I felt quite frightened by the finality of it all.

With 'Bonne Chance' ringing in our ears, we said our farewells and thank yous to our French friends, and headed for the docks. Jimmy told us to pick an unobtrusive spot from which to observe the control point. When we saw some seamen approaching, we were to join them as they went through, keeping as far away as possible from the guard and waving folded pieces of paper of the correct colour. It seemed a very dicey manoeuvre to me, but less unappealing than swimming the river.

About five minutes later a group of five seamen arrived, and a nod from Jimmy confirmed to us that we were to join them when they entered. It went exactly as planned and suddenly we were through and walking towards the berth where our ship would be waiting for us. Throughout our journey, every success had been followed by a setback, and this was no exception. We had been congratulating ourselves on our brilliant success, but when we arrived at the berth where our ship was to be waiting, it wasn't there. Jimmy had mentioned that it had seemed awfully quiet for an area where a ship was due to sail, and now we knew why, but not where the ship had gone. Jimmy's years in the Merchant Navy paid off again; he remembered that ships waiting to sail with the tide were sometimes moved to mooring berths, to leave the loading bays free for other ships. He decided this must be what had happened, so we would have to look nearer the entrance of the docks.

He led us in the direction he reckoned it would be and we began to see signs of life, making it difficult for us to move freely. We could see the masts and funnels of at least three ships ahead of us. If Jimmy was right, one of them would be *Heros*, the one we were looking for. Joe was the first to spot the guard patrolling the quayside. Our problem was how to get near enough to identify which was the one that we wanted – if it was there at all.

32

Despite strict blackout restrictions, there were lights along the dockside where the three ships were lying. The lighting wasn't brilliant but it was still going to make it difficult for us tonight. Railway lines ran the length of the dockside, so we retired to the shelter of some wagons near the ships. We talked over our plan of action and decided that, to save time, we would split up and each find out the name of a ship. Jimmy would take the one on the left, Joe the one on the right, and I got the middle one, which was actually the easy one. Thankfully it was a mild and cloudy night which meant, of course, that away from the lighting it was really dark. This would help cover our movements to a certain extent. When we were having our talk together about the quayside lighting, it had suddenly dawned on us that if there had been no lighting, we wouldn't have been able to identify the ships or see their names.

Our movements now had to coincide with where the patrolling guard was, so the one nearest to him stayed put and the other two had a bit of freedom. I decided that the best place would be under the railway wagons nearest to the ship. As I was crawling along beneath one of these, there was a sudden bump and the wagon started to move. My immediate reaction was to drape myself across the wheel axle which was quite near me, thinking that I would be safe there until the shunter stopped, when I could resume my crawling routine. The result of this was that I was whipped right over the axle and landed on my head, which luckily isn't the weakest part of my body, ending up flat on my back on the track. Before I had gathered my wits, the wagons were stationary again. This little incident taught me that the wheels and axle on this wagon were fixed and did not work independently.

The lighting seemed better at the stern of the ship so I made my way there with an eye on the guard. Eventually, I made out some queer name that looked Russian or Polish, but it wasn't the one we wanted. Returning to the rendezvous point was much easier and quicker. I was becoming better with practice and had a sore head to prove it. The biggest surprise was that the boys were already back and waiting for me. That seemed strange as they had both had further to go than me. I began to wonder if the axle business had knocked me out for a few minutes.

Jimmy had hit the jackpot in the 'find the *Heros* competition', so we moved further back from the quayside towards the ship at the end of the line which, presumably, would be the first one out in the morning when the tide was right. We found a suitable spot in the darkness from which to watch the progress of the guard as he paced his beat on the dockside. Jimmy told us what the plan of action would be. He would wait until the guard was about halfway down his beat with his back to us; then he would walk over to the ship and board it. If all went well, he would signal to us that we were next, but we would follow only after the guard had returned and was again halfway down in the other direction.

There was a deadly stillness about the place, except for the odd bursts of activity from the shunting engine. It was two o'clock in the morning and people were in bed sleeping soundly. Again I fleetingly wondered if we would ever achieve the luxury of sleeping peacefully or in our own beds again. My reverie was rudely shattered when Jimmy said he was off. As he casually walked out into the light and across to the ship's gangway, I imagined rifle and machine-gun fire suddenly sweeping the dockside, but in fact nothing happened. Jimmy disappeared momentarily as he crossed the deck but very quickly reappeared higher up the ship, where he turned round and gave us the thumbs-up sign. Now Joe and I had to wait until the guard had returned and was again halfway down his beat. Time passed too quickly for me, as I felt safe and secure in the dark surroundings, but a touch on my arm put an end to that and we were off.

I felt sure that the guard would hear the thumping of my heart from where he was. Then we were climbing the gangway and all seemed to be going well, until Fate blew the whistle again. From somewhere on our left a voice hailed us and we saw the German guard on deck about twenty yards away. I almost imagined it was the little guard who had played cat and mouse with us on the train. Once again the years of working together paid off. Without even thinking about it, Joe and I both pulled our imaginary passes out of our pockets and waved them in the air, shouting 'Crew' in German, and carried on to where Jimmy was waiting to pull us into a doorway, which he smartly closed behind us. The three of us now stood with bated breath, waiting to see what would happen next.

Nothing did, and Jimmy reckoned that when he came on board the guard must have gone for a pee and that was why he saw no-one. He commended us on how well we had handled a nasty situation. Our next step was decided for us because the door that we had come in by was opened by what looked like a cabin-boy. He didn't look unduly perturbed when he saw us, but this soon changed when he found we were strangers. Jimmy quietly and firmly explained that he was to go and tell the steward that he had met 'Joe Bloggs' in the pub and that he was to come to us immediately. He did this using voice and sign language successfully; when he was finished, the young man indicated that he understood and repeated the message in Swedish, I think.

He went off briskly, closing the door behind him, and now we had a big discussion as to what he would do. I reckoned he would turn us in to my little friend, the guard who was going to haunt me for the rest of my life. Joe was willing to bet his first stop would be one of the ship's officers, but Jimmy just smiled and said the boy would do exactly as he was instructed. Anyway, we would know soon enough – the next time the door was opened. The young man must have moved very fast because about seven minutes later he returned and, thank God, Jimmy was right.

Jimmy's friend arrived alone and seemed dismayed about the three of us having made it this far. But he was as good as his word and in a strangled voice urged us to move very quickly because the whole crew would be on the move soon, preparing the ship for sailing. With him leading the way, we carefully and quietly followed him. This nightmare journey took us deeper and deeper into the ship's bowels. Eventually, we were ushered through yet another bulkhead door, but this proved to be the last one, and it was the coal-bunker. Our final instruction from our Swedish friend was to get into the bunker and as far away from the bulkhead door as possible, then to bury ourselves under the coal and to stay there quietly for as long as possible. We thanked him profusely and genuinely from our hearts, because his help could have cost him his life if we were caught. He smiled warmly at us, wished us 'Bon Voyage' and then he was gone. It made me wonder why a total stranger would put his life on the line for people he didn't know and would probably never see again. I hope that I am never put to the test, in case my moral courage is not a match for his.

The small torch, which I had kept when we dumped everything else, now became very useful and allowed us to see our way to the farthest part of the bunker. On reaching the bulkhead, we began the task of digging ourselves in. Before we started, Jimmy said that he had something to tell us. It was extremely likely that the Germans would search the ship before it sailed by one of two methods. One was using dogs to sniff out any human scent in cargo holds and the second, a real charmer, was using gas instead of the dogs. This, of course, cheered us up no end.

It was the bad-following-the-good syndrome again. Here we were, having surmounted all sorts of obstacles to get this far, to be told we would either have our throats torn out by Alsatian dogs or be asphyxiated instead. I suggested that possibly our only way out was by prayer, but Joe said that it was hardly fair to ask for help now, considering the situation we had put ourselves in. Jimmy said we should leave it in the hands of Lady Luck, who had looked after us inordinately well up till now, and since we hadn't offended her in any way, maybe she would see us through.

Short of crying and screaming that we didn't want to die, there was nothing else for it but to dig ourselves into the coal. Jimmy explained we were doing this to cover our scent from the dogs, and I was glad there was a reason because it wasn't an easy task with bare hands. We had only been resting for about ten minutes after our exertions when there was a bump and the coal moved under us. Jimmy told us we would have to move as we were obviously lying right above the hopper that fed the ship's furnaces. When you're in trouble there is no greater therapy than keeping yourself occupied, so we moved and did our digging-in chore all over again.

Half an hour later, while I was daydreaming about walking to birdsong along one of our beautiful lochsides in the warm sunshine, Jimmy suddenly said that the ship was moving, which brought me back to reality. I hadn't even heard the engines starting but was told that they had been ticking over for some time and we were now definitely under way. Jimmy explained that it was quite some distance before we would sail clear of the estuary and that the ship's search would be carried out while we were on the move. The ship's pilot, the guards and any stowaways that were found would be taken off the ship when they dropped the pilot. His predictions were spot on: ten minutes later we heard a dog, first whining then barking, followed by the angry voice of the guard shouting at the dog to be quiet. The sound must have come to us through a ventilator which we couldn't see. I'm sure the dog had got a whiff of us and was telling its master about us down below. For some reason the guard didn't want to know.

Then I had another thought. Supposing the guard knew the holds were going to be gassed, then of course he wouldn't be interested in the dog's reaction to any smells coming from the ventilators – be it German or Swedish rats, or even, as in this case, three Britons. This supposition would make a dramatic and final end to our relationship with the little guard from the train. Having exchanged thoughts and fears in whispers, we decided to wait and see what would happen next. We once again settled down to contemplating our filthy navels.

My nerves must have stopped jumping long enough to allow me to doze off. I was awakened by Jimmy and Joe talking quite freely together, and when they saw I was back in the land of the living they told me that we were well clear of the estuary and heading safely for Sweden and the port of Malmö. The sense of elation that swept through me almost knocked me out. All the planning and dreaming we had done together had finally ended in success. Then, as we hugged each other, waves of fear started to run up and down my spine. Jimmy felt the sudden tension in my body and asked me what was wrong. I felt almost sick as I reminded him of the pattern of events: very soon Fate was going to throw that rotten sucker punch which had followed every time we thought we were winning. Both boys laughed and told me to forget it; nothing could interfere with a safe landing in Malmö. I agreed to set aside my pessimism and behave myself, but deep down in the pit of my stomach the fear remained. Maybe it was just hunger.

33

A couple of hours later, we thought it was about time to make our presence on board known to the Captain, as Jimmy reckoned we had passed the point of no return. At the same time, the bulk-head door swung open and the lights were switched on. There stood one of the ship's officers, presumably checking all was well in the coal-hole. Being naturally polite, we called out a hearty 'Good morning' to him. His look of shocked surprise was understandable: we must have looked dreadful in our filthy state. When we explained to him that we were British stowaways, he smiled and said that he could understand English and that he would take us to the Captain. He also explained that the 'Old Man' was a real seagoing terror and that he would be furious with us for our audacity in stowing away on his ship.

He took us up on deck and told us to wait. His prediction was spot on. The Captain appeared at the double, hoping that what he had been told wasn't true, but when he saw us he realised that the worst had happened and that he would now be in trouble with the Germans. He was no beauty to start with, and as his tough wrinkled face got redder by the minute, he became more ugly. First he tongue-lashed us in Swedish, then he switched to English, the main theme being that if ever there was anyone in the world he didn't want to meet, it was definitely us. Our reaction to all this was mutual. We said nothing because, after all, it was his ship and he was entitled to his say – not that any of us felt like interrupting him in the mood he was in.

When he finally ran out of breath, he had a good look around and then he asked the ship's officer (who had been standing by during this tirade) if it was possible to chart him a course for Denmark, which was German-occupied. If he dropped us there, he would be in the clear again and we would be recaptured. Leaving us standing there on deck, the two of them retired to the bridge, whereupon Jimmy had a good look around at the direction we were heading. He told us that the land we could see straight ahead was Sweden and the dimmer bit to the left Denmark, so if the present course altered to the left we were to jump overboard and take our chances on swimming for Sweden. We both nodded in agreement. I think Jimmy might have made it; Joe might not have, but for me it would have been a watery grave for sure.

We were left standing on deck for about fifteen minutes before the friendly officer returned and, with a wink, told us to follow him. He showed us where to wash up and then we could have a meal. Our course as we left the deck was still straight and true, so we smiled at each other and felt a lot better about life. We washed and scrubbed but five minutes later we were dirty again. I thought I would probably spend the rest of my life trying to get rid of the coal dust, but in fact it took only about a week. A friendly cook in the seamen's mess served us with a lovely meaty-smelling soup, which was absolutely delicious. The nice man couldn't understand when he tried to serve us with a heaped main course that we were full and couldn't eat another bite. He looked so disappointed that we went to a lot of trouble to explain to him that after four years on strict rations, our stomachs wouldn't hold a lot, no matter how good and tasty the food was. Finally he accepted that it wasn't his cooking that was the problem and grudgingly cleared the table.

We were left in the mess-room to sit and chat and wonder

what was going to happen next. What happened was that practically the whole crew appeared in ones and twos at various times to give us encouraging smiles and the thumbs-up sign. They were probably surprised that the Captain hadn't had us put in irons and thrown in the brig. A regular check on our course showed that we were still heading straight and true for Sweden and the coastline was becoming quite distinct now. It was a beautiful sunny day and we could make out features on land. The officer who had been dealing with us visited us about an hour later and said he would have to have some details from us. There were forms to be filled in for the ship's log. These proved to be just generalities, like names and addresses and a statement that no-one had helped us to stow away on this particular ship. He informed us that the Swedish police had been notified by radio of our presence on board and would be waiting at the dockside to pick us up when we landed at Malmö.

Two hours later, that is exactly what happened. Two well-dressed civilians came on board as soon as the ship was tied up and the one in charge advised us to say nothing until after we had accompanied them to their office in town. The Captain didn't show up to wave goodbye to us, though we would have liked to thank him for his hospitality and our safe delivery to Sweden.

The two CID men were most charming, producing cups of tea for us when we arrived at their office. Then the most amazing interview took place; we were told that we must think very carefully before answering any of the questions we were about to be asked, as our fate for the rest of the war would depend on our answers. They explained that if we declared ourselves to be members of the armed forces, the authorities would have to place us in an internment camp in Sweden until the cessation of hostilities. If, and if was a very big if, on the other hand we were to declare ourselves as civilians, then we would be handed over to the British Consul in Malmö and the Swedish authorities would wash their hands of us.

Here was an interesting choice: to see out the rest of the war in a neutral country, nice and safe, or get back home and risk the possibility of getting killed or maimed properly this time. Were we going to trade one camp for another, or complete the task we had set out to achieve and get home? It might take some people a day, a week, maybe longer to weigh up the pros and cons, but it took the three of us about thirty seconds. Jimmy looked at us and said 'Mister' and Joe and I nodded in agreement. We were registered as civilians, and gave our names and addresses, whereupon the British Consul was immediately notified and we were picked up within the hour.

The three of us gleefully hugged each other and found it hard to believe that it was finally over. All the future planning was out of our hands and had become someone else's problem. Our part of the escape was now successfully completed.

34

The Consul was a young-old man, very civil service, who gave us the impression that we had interrupted him, and that he would deal with us only because it was his duty. Our first stop was at his office, where he did a very intensive report on our personal details and then a less thorough summary of our escape. When this was completed, he arranged for a light snack to be delivered to the office.

After this we were told that we were going shopping. The car drove us to a gents' outfitters which looked very genteel and upmarket. Only when we got inside did we realise just how posh it really was.

The next hour was a fairytale come true and a dream I would love to relive. We were told to choose a whole new wardrobe without giving any thought to expense and that the costs of our three outfits would be borne by the King of Sweden, God bless him.

We must have made a ludicrous sight, still dressed in our filthy old clothes. We started by picking our suits. I chose a brownish two-piece sports suit, then a smart pair of brown shoes to go with it. Coats and hats followed, then two shirts each to match our individual outfits, two pair of socks, a tie and a belt, then two sets of underwear and two sets of pyjamas. Then we had to choose a suitcase to put everything in. Slightly breathless, we reckoned that nothing had been forgotten but we were reminded that we had to choose a full toilet set with nothing left out. This done, we were told there was still something missing and were taken to another department to choose a wristwatch and a pair of cufflinks each. I hope His Majesty received our 'Thank you' cards – the Consul assured us that he would.

Next stop was a quiet hotel overlooking the water. I couldn't believe they would let us in looking as we did, but they were waiting for us and we were shown to our rooms and informed that our baths were already drawn. All we had to do was soak in them. After what we had been through in the last few weeks, not to mention the last few years, it was sheer unadulterated luxury. It also felt extremely strange: for the first time in almost five years I was completely alone.

I took full advantage of it now by bathing, shaving and dressing slowly and alone. Finally I went through to Jimmy's room just as Joe was also arriving. We all looked at each other in amazement – three strangers in civilian clothes – then we all howled with laughter and the spell was broken. We had opted for a quiet dinner in the hotel by ourselves. Next day we were going north to Stockholm by train. There we would be taken to the home of the British Military Attaché, where we would stay until further notice – whatever that meant. Dinner was a gastronomic dream and we actually managed to eat three of the five courses, though we insisted on very small portions. After a cup of tea in the lounge, we chatted a bit, but the comfortable-looking beds upstairs were acting like big magnets, so we decided on an early night – which turned out to be a mistake.

Next morning when we met for breakfast, we found that not one of us had had the pleasure of a good night's sleep. Like myself, Jimmy and Joe had tossed and turned all night, going over the last stages of our journey and trying to figure out where the German system had gone wrong and why we had succeeded against the odds. Why were we not picked up in Sagan station? Why didn't the little guard spot our phoney documents on the train? How could we have entered a guarded dock area and then board a guarded ship without being caught? Round and round it went, then a desperate effort to shut it all out, then a few seconds later round and round it would go again – and so it went on through the restless night.

We all felt much better and cheerier after a sumptuous breakfast, and shortly afterwards we were told that a car was waiting to take us to the station. Our cases had already been brought down so, having been given pocket money, we tipped the porter and joined the Consul in the car. He was very sympathetic about our sleepless night but agreed that this phase would surely pass. Our minds just needed to adjust to our new lifestyle. He gave us our tickets for the journey and some more money, which he said we would need for the buffet car on the train. We thought this was very thoughtful of him. He told us that we would be picked up on arrival at Stockholm. After an uneventful train journey a driver came forward and checked we were the correct trio before driving us through this remarkably clean and beautiful city to the Attaché's house, where we were greeted by three lovely ladies and the man himself.

Mr Wright was a middle-aged, handsome man's man. I'm sure if he hadn't been in the job he was in, he would have fitted into the Diplomatic Corps nicely. A few minutes after meeting him you felt that he would be able to solve any problems that you had and that you could confide in him safely. His wife complemented him beautifully. Over the period that we stayed with them she was charming, motherly and quite flawless. The two daughters, one brunette and one blonde, were in their early twenties and both quite capable of turning any man's head. Considering the number of years we had been deprived of any type of female company (apart from my forays to Traudl), this was indeed an excess of feminine beauty to place before us, but what with Jimmy and Joe being happily married and faithful husbands and me being more or less spoken for, we just tried to regard the ladies as ordinary people, which was very difficult.

After we were shown to our rooms in this large but comfortable old house, our host called us to his office where, for the next couple of hours, we underwent a most thorough interrogation, firstly about our home lives, then our army careers, and the time we spent in prison camp, culminating finally in our escape. It all seemed excessive, but then slowly I realised that he was trying to establish whether we were who we claimed to be. In short, it was possible we were plants.

Suddenly, I almost went off the nice gentleman. He asked if we still had the identity cards that I had made, and when we produced them he gave them a cursory glance and said that we were fortunate not to have had them examined as they were pretty poor copies. When we told him that they had been checked by a Control on the train, he laughed and said that we must be joking. When we insisted that it was true, he was astounded. I felt awful at his ridicule, after all the work I had done on the damn things, but on second thoughts I felt better, because without them we wouldn't have been there.

When Jimmy told his story of his visit to the pub in Stettin, our host broke out in hilarious laughter. He then explained that the barmaid who had tried to chat him up was a British agent called Mary, and that if he had given her a chance she would have taken over and arranged our passage to Sweden the easy way.

He then went on to say that we had coincidentally taken an official route for our escape and, though we were Civil Service personnel and therefore covered by the Official Secrets Act, under no circumstances could we disclose the route we had taken to anyone without government permission. It could jeopardise lives if it became common knowledge.

The next piece of news that he gave us was quite shocking and meant that our sleepless nights might go on for some time yet. Unconfirmed news had come through to him that fifty of the airmen who had escaped from Sagan had been caught and, unbelievably, they had all been shot on direct orders from Hitler passed through Heinrich Himmler. He told us that the total number of men involved in the escape had been in excess of sixty. My first thought was, what kind of so-called Escape Committee sends so many men out into a hostile environment with very little hope of success? To my mind it was a wanton and completely irresponsible action and one that had no hope of achieving anything. Jimmy and Joe never agreed with me on this.

After the bad news came the good. We would be issued next day with covering letters of identity, which we could produce on request, and we could write to our next-of-kin informing them that we had arrived safely in Sweden and, with any luck, would be home in the near future. We couldn't tell them exactly where we were in Sweden. Joe then sent a postcard to Danny back in the Jagerndorf camp to say that we were safely through. Incidentally, apparently the guards never found out how we managed to get out of that barrack-room, and a special squad was sent in to investigate – but they had no success either, so it remained a mystery. Danny did such a good job on those bars that he should have got a medal too. I sent a postcard to one of our friends in Lamsdorf asking him to thank the Escape Committee in Stalag VIIIB for their non-co-operation. I never found out if they received the message.

We were told we would eventually be airlifted back to the UK and must be on standby, ready to move out at any moment. During the course of our stay the family was visited by two RAF officers wearing BOAC uniforms. Apparently they flew in and out of Stockholm to collect the diplomatic mail. Their aircraft were unmarked Mosquito bombers, unarmed so that they didn't break the Geneva

Convention rules. Not to be outdone, the Germans used the same system but they used Messerschmidts, which were also unmarked and unarmed to fly between Stockholm and Berlin. All very nice and proper, but both sides had a little game of guessing when these particular aircraft would be in the air, and real fighter planes would stooge around and try to shoot them down, with a fair rate of success on both sides.

The next few weeks were spent on a social round of invitations to both British and Swedish homes. We had often heard of the higher standard of living in Sweden but it had to be seen to be believed. Time flew pleasantly by and we slowly recuperated and became fairly normal people again, though we all still had difficulty in sleeping properly. Time was the only cure for this.

One beautiful summer morning John Wright told us that the Invasion had begun and this was the news the whole world was waiting for. We were now on Red Alert to fly home, so we had to be packed and ready to go at any moment. Twenty-four hours later Joe was the first to be taken to the airport and sent home. Jimmy and I were to go on the following day but in separate aircraft. When our turn came I was highly excited as we dressed up in flying suits and then donned a parachute harness. Jimmy and I then parted to go on our separate bombers. I was given quick instructions on how to plug in the oxygen mask and transmitter and told not to talk over the intercom as the pilot and navigator wanted no interference on this channel while flying. There was a wire mesh cage fitted in the bomb-bay and this could be raised and lowered to carry the mail. Now came the crunch. I was told not to put my parachute pack on to the harness, as I wouldn't be able to get into the bomb-bay if I was wearing it. There wasn't enough space. I was to push my pack in first and then climb in.

After I was in and had located my plug-in point, the horrible truth dawned on me – I didn't need a parachute because there was no way I could possibly wear it if anything happened. This actually wasn't quite true; I could wear it as long as I stayed in the plane. The bomb-bay doors closed and the pilot came on the intercom to check that I was OK and reminded me that I was on radio silence until we arrived home.

In the dark I thought over our sudden parting from the Wright family and how hospitable and friendly they had been. We had become extremely fond of them and would miss them. These thoughts were soon interrupted by the roar of twin engines warming up. A few minutes later we were airborne. Listening to what was going on between the pilot and the navigator was a revelation. Everything was being done at top speed. The idea was to get up as high as possible in the shortest time, and when this point was reached, it was a high-speed dive straight down to Scotland. The intercom was alive with staccato bursts of talk – was that something? How about over there? Above? Something caught my eye … no, not there, over to the left. All the time I was hoping that the Luftwaffe would be too busy on the new front to worry about us.

35

It didn't seem to be very long before the pitch of the engines changed to a less menacing tone and, as if in harmony with this, the voices of the crew became less tense. Subconsciously, it also had an effect on me, as I was now able to stop my fingernails biting into the palms of my hands, though I had been completely unaware of this until I relaxed.

Although I could see nothing outside, my stomach told me quite clearly that we had started to dive towards Scotland. Now, for the first time, I started to wonder how Jimmy was doing in his Mosquito and if he had worked out how much good his parachute would be in the case of accidents. This train of thought was soon ended as the crew began to radio in for landing instructions. We were soon bumping along the runway at Leuchars. When we finally came to a standstill, the bomb-bay doors were silently opened and the infernal wire basket was lowered and I was able to throw out my parachute pack before clambering out onto the runway. A truck was waiting to collect the diplomatic mail but I was told to stand by and within a few minutes the plane carrying my big brother landed and finally rolled to a stop near ours.

Jimmy scrambled out and after a big congratulatory success hug we made our way together to the flight office. Here, after getting out of all the flying paraphernalia, we heartily and profusely thanked our respective crews and wished them luck for the future. Unfortunately, this didn't do them much good; we heard later from Sweden that my crew were shot down and killed about six weeks later. Naturalists wonder what drives the lemmings to their suicidal rush to their deaths over cliffs into the sea, but what about the men who enter a war where the odds are stacked against them? Many times in prison camp I thought about what I would do if we ever got home safely, and the recurring answer was that never again would they get me into a situation that didn't correspond with the job I had signed up to do.

Why should a signalman like myself end up lying behind a bren gun on a road block, when his commander-in-chief and all his elite troops were on a ship heading for home? How was it that some people had done so much better? For example, a friend of mine, also a signalman in our line section, was on the same assignment with Joe and me when we ended up in Bolougne and were diverted to the road block. He worked it out and decided that this wasn't why he was in France, and so he slung his hook and headed for home where he was, of course, welcomed as a Dunkirk hero. Believe it or not, by the time we arrived home in 1944 he was a major in the Royal Signals and the three of us were still signalmen. So much for desertion in the face of the enemy and getting your just deserts.

An officer from Military Intelligence came forward and introduced himself. He told us that we would have to go through the whole rigmarole of how, where and when again, but it seemed to get easier each time and he kept the information he required to a minimum. I have to admit that I couldn't tell you his name or what he looked like, and when he stopped me several weeks later in the Intelligence Depot in Wentworth to ask how I was, I had no recollection of having met him before. He said this was understandable as Jimmy and I were quite overwrought on our arrival from Sweden.

When our debriefing session was finally over, we were passed to the Duty Officer for his attention. What we fervently hoped for was a rail warrant to Glasgow but this hope was quickly dashed. We were told to proceed under escort to the War Office in London for some real interrogation by the experts who were waiting for us. Apparently only about a dozen British POWs had reached Sweden since the beginning of the war, so we made up twenty-five percent of this figure, which wasn't bad going for three lads from Glasgow

Jimmy and I had been in touch with big brother William, who was the only one in the family with a telephone in his home. Only now could we tell him where we were and where we were going next. The family couldn't understand why we weren't allowed to return to Glasgow rather than travel south to London. We couldn't answer this question, and personally I was beginning to think in terms of another escape. All we wanted was to go home, see our family and sleep in our own beds, but for the moment this was impossible.

Instead, after a meal and early bed we had to catch the first train in the morning to Edinburgh and travel with our escort to London. We were promised that after the London debriefing we would finally be allowed to go home. This still seemed awfully remote, and not at all as we had pictured our homecoming.

36

Luckily for us, we had seats reserved on the train, otherwise we would have had to join the crowd of service and civilian travellers who had to sit on their suitcases and various other forms of luggage in the crowded corridors of the Edinburgh-London express. We were being escorted in the nicest possible way to our debriefing session with the Intelligence personnel of the three services about our successful escape from the POW camp.

The three of us were beginning to feel tired and edgy. When you consider that in the morning we had been in Sweden, then flown to Scotland in Mosquito bombers, and were now heading for London in an overcrowded train, this was perhaps understandable. Jimmy O'Neill, my brother, Joe Harkin, my friend, and John McCallum, myself, were hitting a very low ebb after the euphoria of our big success. If we hadn't been so spoiled in Sweden, maybe it wouldn't have been so bad, but coming down to earth with such a big bang was difficult.

If all politicians had to suffer hardship and deprivation after a war was declared, then there would be no more war; talking is easy and cheap, but you still need the silly sods who will go out and do the dirty work for the professional talkers. If the cabinet ministers who declare a state of war were forced to operate from the front line then, as they promised in the two world wars, we would indeed all be home for Christmas. It's strange the thoughts that run through your head when you're suffering from a major anticlimax.

Halfway into England we managed to get a cup of tea and some sandwiches from a trolley at one of the stations we stopped at, and although we complained about the quality, we were grateful to be able to get them at all. As we moved further south, we were shocked at what we saw on the roads. An interminable array of all sorts of tanks and other armoured vehicles were parked along sections of the main roads along with thousands of trucks of all kinds and weights.

My mind went back to the day the efficient German army had rolled past me on the road block outside Bolougne; I had felt sorry for our troops behind me, knowing what they had to face. Now the boot was on the other foot and I could almost sympathise with the enemy, knowing the scale of the equipment that was ready to engage them. Strange pictures and thoughts were racing through my mind. They were brought to an abrupt end as Jimmy shook me awake and told me we were in London.

By the time we had consumed a greasy breakfast in the dingy station restaurant, I was once again fully awake. I was expecting to see the horrific damage that London had suffered at the hands of the Luftwaffe, but the crafty cab driver took a devious route that showed none of this. London looked like a normal bustling metropolitan city as we passed through. Our strictly anonymous escort quickly arranged our security passes at the reception desk in the War Office and handed us over to another escort. We were taken through a maze of corridors and finally arrived at a door which mysteriously opened. Our escort ushered us in and closed the door behind us. Here, we were suddenly greeted by real people again.

Representatives of the three Armed Services interviewed us, each being interested in different things, and extracted information from us that we had no idea we had. The RAF intelligence officer made notes of the fact that the lovely big red Post Office building still stood untouched in the middle of Stettin. By the look on his face this would not be the case for very long. The Navy were naturally interested in what we had seen in the dock area. Military intelligence had the hardest job as their interest stretched from 1939 until now, the middle of 1944. Eventually we were squeezed dry and they handed us over to an officer who would arrange our proper documentation, plus pay, plus leave, plus rail warrants for our journey home and back to a reporting camp on the termination of our leave.

When the smug captain stated that we would be granted twenty-eight days' leave and would then return to the army selection unit designated on our leave passes, it all started to go wrong. I politely interrupted and asked him to repeat the number of days of leave. This he promptly did, whereupon I informed him that as far as I was concerned this was completely unacceptable and nowhere near the amount of accrued leave we were due for the last five years. Can you imagine – the Dunkirk fiasco, four years in POW, you make your own way home – and you're told you can have five and a half days' leave for every year that you were away. I asked the good captain if he could tell me exactly how many days' leave he had had in the last five years, at which point he threatened to bring in the sergeant-major and have me arrested for insubordination.

Jimmy realised I had gone too far and told me to be quiet and give the officer a chance to clarify the situation, which he did. He told us that if at the end of twenty-eight days we felt we needed more time to adjust, then we should ring him and he would make the necessary arrangements. Why he couldn't have said that in the first place I don't know, though it is possible that I didn't give him a chance. The paperwork was duly completed and, after a few nasty looks, we parted company. Now our target was home.

We finally settled down in the northbound train from Euston which, like the last train we were on, was overcrowded. I now had time to think some loving thoughts about Traudl and try to come up with some way of letting her know what had happened since we had parted company. The three of us discussed the problem and always came up with the same answer. Any attempt to get in touch with her would compromise her safety and wellbeing. It seemed ironic that we could inform Stalag VIIIB of our success but couldn't tell Traudl. I felt if we had discussed it with her before we left, she would probably have come up with a solution to the problem.

Perhaps the reason we had never discussed it was that, in my heart, I had never really believed we would succeed. I did ask advice from the Foreign Office later. They said there was nothing anyone could do at this stage of the war. So, for the present, it was a case of putting it out of my mind, which I didn't find easy.

37

After another rude awakening I was told that we were approaching Glasgow. I began to wonder if I was going to spend the rest of my life dropping off to sleep. Strangely enough, to this day I only have to close my eyes and I can doze off, even standing up. It may have some connection to the severe nervous attacks I had developed, even though these were occurring less and less – thank God, as they were still terrifying when they happened.

Outside the station we said goodbye to Joe for the present and arranged when we would meet again. Then Jimmy and I shared a taxi as we lived quite close to each other. Glasgow didn't look any different after years of war, and soon we were in Maryhill and I was kissing my sister-in-law Clara 'hello and goodbye'. A few minutes later the taxi was turning into the street where my mother lived. Flags and bunting and 'Welcome Home John' banners were strung all over the place and surprised me because I had never been very familiar with any of the neighbours. Most of them would never have recognised me under normal circumstances, but now they knew what I looked like because of the newspaper stories and photographs.

The family re-union doesn't have to be described, but was certainly memorable. No-one seemed to think it strange, though, that in twenty-eight days we would be expected to enter the fray again. With what results next time, I wondered? I thought of asking them to alter the banners to read 'Welcome Home John – for twenty-eight days'.

During the four years we had been in POW camp we had all assumed that if or when we returned to the UK the war would be over for us. But here we were, faced with the possibility of doing another five years, perhaps even longer. What we had heard in London was that the army was delighted we were back because tradesmen of our calibre were at a premium and that we would be back in service with as little delay as possible. What they didn't know was that at least one tradesman had no intention of going back to the Royal Signals to start all over again. In 1937 I had enlisted in the Reservists in this rank and now in 1944 my rank was still the same. My gut feeling was that there must be something else that I could do in the army that would give me promotion virtually immediately, and when I returned to duty this would be my top priority.

On the surface everything looked the same in Glasgow but things were very different when you moved around. I went into a tobacconist's in Maryhill Road two days later and, without thinking, casually asked the nice old grey-haired man behind the counter for twenty Players. First he looked at me as if I had come from another planet, then he thought over what I had asked for and finally he burst into hilarious laughter. While he was still laughing I went outside the shop and checked the sign above the door to make sure I was in the right establishment. Then I re-entered and repeated my request for twenty Players. When he calmed down, he asked me where I had been hiding for the last few years. After hearing my story, he realised I was one of the three he had read about in the papers, and went on to explain that good cigarettes were at a premium and hard to come by unless you were in the good books of your friendly tobacconist. Then the kind old gentleman produced the said cigarettes from behind the counter and promised that while I was on leave I could have twenty Players every day. Needless to say, we became good friends.

38

Suddenly I had fan mail. But when mother said that I would have to answer it all, the fun of being famous evaporated. I compromised by placing a 'thank you' ad in the newspapers. Then the neighbours organised a presentation dance in the church hall. The presentation that they made was a leather wallet containing money which had been collected for me. I was supposed to make a speech, but I was completely incapable of doing so. As far as I remember I muttered something about 'thanks a million' and sat down. Reporters came and went and one of them even tried to buy the snap-brim soft hat that I had got in Sweden – with no success, I may add.

I had three weeks of going to bed when I felt like it and, even more important, not getting up in the morning until I wanted to, staying in or going out just as I pleased, and all this without armed guards controlling my movements. It seemed too good to be true. We had just spent almost five years in uniform, at all times under the command of someone else in uniform, never having any say in what we were going to do next, nor when we were going to do it.

We had often dreamed and fantasised about how wonderful it would be to be back in the way of life we were now leading, but that was when we thought it would never happen. But it had, and now after three weeks of inactivity, I realised I was bored and unhappy. Mother did her best by suggesting people I should go and visit. This unfortunately didn't solve my problem and it was almost with relief that I realised that in a few days we would be heading south again to start all over again.

Within myself, I knew it was a very different person starting out this time. I may not have been a better person, but I was much harder and definitely more ambitious. After the usual tearful and sad farewells to the family, the three of us met and set out on the next phase of our adventures, wondering how and when this part would end.

39

The Army Selection Training Unit (ASTU) that we had to report to was new and foreign to our previous experience of army discipline. As telephone engineers we were skilled tradesmen, and had been treated with a certain respect, to the extent of being allowed a great deal of laxity in matters of drill and square-bashing and even dress. In this new establishment we were lumped together with rejects from other units, misfits and new recruits. The idea was to classify and put a qualification tag on the finished article. Individually, we might have come to grief in this place, but as a team we managed to stay out of trouble and kept ourselves to ourselves as far as possible. This wasn't always easy, as a lot of the troublemakers were trying to get out of the army altogether.

I came to grief very quickly and it happened very simply. We had just finished eating our main meal in the mess-hall on the second day there and I was about to scrape my plate clean in the swill-bin when the duty sergeant-major screamed at me, asking what I thought I was doing. Politely I explained that I couldn't eat any more. Presumably the bins would be collected and the contents used as pig-swill, so it wouldn't go to waste. I thought this would mollify him but it seemed to have the opposite effect. He became livid and I thought he was going to burst. He began to scream again, asking if I realised that thousands of merchant seamen had died to get that food to us and here was an unworthy sod scraping it into the swill-bin as if it grew on trees. I tried to explain that there had only been a tiny bit left on the plate and that I was very sorry about the seamen, but his rage continued. He took my name, rank and number and put me on a charge for wasting food. Since signing on in 1937 I had never been on a charge, and here I was in 1944 being put on a one by a big ugly bastard who had never been out of the country and for five years had been eating and drinking at the expense of the army.

The following morning I was marched into the duty officer and the charge read out. When I explained that my stomach had shrunk and under what circumstances, the charge was dropped and I was marched out again. So I still had a clean sheet. My priority for the remainder of the time spent in this camp was to keep as far away as possible from the sergeant-major. Fortunately I managed this and no further incidents occurred.

After we had been whipped into shape physically, we were assessed on our individual ability to use our brainpower. The result was a mass of very quick postings. The Mensa tests and the Morse code recognition tests created havoc and the assessments were soon made.

Jimmy and Joe were posted to the Royal Signals Depot at Catterick. This was to be our final parting in the army and it turned out to be quite emotional, which was not at all surprising after all we had been through in the past five years. Before they left we received official word that we had been awarded Military Medals for our recent achievement. We had been told that this would probably happen but when it did it was a nice highlight to the last few gruelling months and years! Our battledress tunics were taken to the regimental tailor and were soon returned with three lovely medal ribbons stitched on the chest. They were the ribbons of the MM, the 1939–43 Star as it then was, and the Territorial Medal for twelve years' service (which we wouldn't have been entitled to except that the war years counted double). I had an extra embellishment in the form of a gold vertical stripe on my left forearm, showing that I had been wounded in action. I always kept my hand over the ribbons if the sergeant-major was anywhere in sight so that I wouldn't antagonise him.

I was pretty lonely after the boys left, but as a counter to this the rest of the course became quite intensive. We always knew when the training was going to get rough or dirty because then we had to parade in denims. If anyone had told me then that they would become a pet hatred, I would never have believed them. I hated them then, and still do.

40

In the middle of the course I was called in to the major's office and asked if I would consider foregoing the trip to Buckingham Palace for the medal presentation. If I would, then he would arrange to have the presentation made by the CO on the barrack square. I readily agreed to this as it suited my retiring nature better.

Eventually the whole course was completed and I was informed that my new category in the army included a note indicating I was a PO3. Just in case this was something nasty and could be held against me, I asked what it meant. It was explained that it was the code for Potential Officer Grade Three. I wonder what I had done wrong to fail Grades One and Two?

Next was the visit to the officer who decided where you went from here. My guardian angel arranged for it to be the nice major I had become fairly friendly with. Earlier in the course he had arranged a trip together on some pretext and had stopped at a restaurant for a very tasty lunch. It dawned on me later that this was partly to see if I knew how to eat properly and wouldn't be an embarrassment in the Mess.

We chatted a little and then he pointed out that there would be no difficulty in disposing of me. I would automatically be returned to the Royal Signals, where it wouldn't take too long to bring me up to date. Quietly I asked if I could tell him a little of what had been going on in my mind over the past few months. He agreed to listen.

In the next few minutes I tried to explain to him how it felt to have signed on as a signalman and be starting all over again five long years later, my rank still the same. My younger brother had volunteered after the war started and was now a corporal in the Signals, and one of the signalmen who had skipped the job on the road-block on which I was wounded and captured was now a full-blown major. Surely he must understand that if this new army and I were going to be compatible there had to be some sort of instant promotion, otherwise I would most likely be returning to No. 1 ASTU as a problem soldier.

When I stopped talking he sat looking at me for some time. Finally he shrugged his shoulders and gave me a rueful smile. He then admitted that if he were to carry out his duty properly, it would be back to the Signals and no arguments. On the other hand it would be intriguing to see if anything could be conjured up to make my dreams come true. He suggested that we should begin by looking at the military manual and seeing what that might produce. I asked if the Military Police would be an option and this was promptly turned down, but it did trigger something in his mind and he remembered that he had a pal in the Intelligence Corps. He began to check the manual for the required qualifications for the IC and the next few minutes would have made a wonderful script for the music halls.

First question – what university or college did you attend? I told him he could stop right there, but the major was in full flight and wanted details. I told him the best we could do was St George's Road AC (Advanced Central), a school I had left aged 14. He said that if we left out the Road and put AC together it would look like Academy, and St George's Academy sounded like a very good school to him.

The next question was – how many languages do you have and with what degree of fluency? I explained to him that although I had been one year in France, I couldn't speak French, but he insisted that I must know a lot of French words. This I couldn't deny, so he summed it up as 'French – fair'. Then he insisted that if I had been four years in Germany I must be fluent. I was honest and said that I wasn't capable of carrying on an intelligent conversation in German. His summing up was 'German – colloquial'.

His next step was to telephone his chum in Wentworth Woodhouse, which was the Intelligence Corps Depot, and after a cosy little chat it was arranged that I would appear there as soon as possible for an interview with their recruiting officer. I thanked this very kind man for his attempt to solve my problem and promised to do my utmost not to let him down.

The interview was a success and I was accepted for training with the new intake. The course turned out to be both rigorous and demanding, physically and mentally, with quite a number of drop-outs, and you emerged as a rather different person. I was posted out to Northern Command to complete my ground training and, operating from Sheffield, part of my security duties included visits to two German POW camps, namely Lodge Moor and Doncaster Racecourse. This was a real turn-up for the book after having done four years in captivity myself. I must say, they were better fed than we were.

41

Our section officer was Captain Philip Haigh, who earlier in the war had been unfortunate enough to encounter a hand grenade, but time had healed the damage. Like my own, his nightmares probably went on for a long time, though increasingly spaced out.

He was a lean, dapper, handsome and well-educated man, naturally cheerful, and he always made you feel you were lucky to be working for him. I asked him one day if it would be on the cards for me to be included in his section if he were ever given a posting to Germany. Without hesitation, he said that if it were at all possible, he would keep me in mind; he was as keen to go there as I was. I didn't tell him about Traudl as it didn't seem relevant yet. The way the war was going, it looked as if I wouldn't get the chance. Monty had been told to stand fast and engage the main resistance of the German army while the Americans were racing in their tanks all over the rest of the country. However, the day came and I was recalled to the Intelligence Depot to be told by Captain Haigh that he had finally been detailed to take a section to Brussels, our Field HQ for Germany.

I was one up on the rest of the section as I had already worked with the boss, but it didn't take long to get acquainted during our kitting-up period. Two of the team were Scots. One was Bob Hunter from Larkhall and the other was Andy Thomson from Glasgow. Bob and I became good friends and later I had the pleasure of being best man at his wedding. He was seconded to Intelligence from the Royal Scots Greys, a very proud horse regiment. To me, Bob always looked and walked like a cowboy. To crown it all, if we were ever out on an assignment, he would fold the cover of his revolver holster in, so that the butt stood out – very effective. Andy was different altogether. Where Bob was dark in complexion, Andy was blonde, and it took a bit longer to get to know him, though we became quite friendly later on.

Our sergeant-major was a taciturn little man and much more mature than the rest of us. I never really got to know him as his main job was administration and, of course, most of the time we were out and about and had little contact with each other. My other friend in the new section was 'Benny' Goodman, who was a little rounder than the rest of us, which perhaps acounted for his very good nature. His proper name was Victor but everyone preferred to call him Benny. On the whole, I felt that the section was fairly well balanced, with a mixture of what I would call hard men and intellectuals. Whether this had been deliberately achieved or not I wouldn't know, but what I did know was that a very great number of security sections would be required for the occupation of Germany when the capitulation came.

We had been allocated to the MI8 side of the business, which covered port and frontier security. I was hoping for some remote frontier where I could maybe have a chance to contact Traudl.

The section was finally kitted out and we had only to collect our vehicles. As everyone had to be mobile you were either allocated a 30-hundredweight truck or a motorbike. Andy and I were on the bike squad. Along with some others we went off to collect our machines, which turned out to be beautiful gleaming new BSA 500s. My joy at seeing them was short-lived as they were immediately spray painted with horrible camouflage green. There was an almost conciliatory bonus when I learned that Andy was an expert mechanic and specialised in motorbikes. He proved this many times over in the period that we were together. Any tuning or adjustments that he made on his bike were duplicated on mine. The captain, of course, got the ubiquitous Jeep with a driver called Paddy thrown in for good measure. As his name implied, he hailed from the Emerald Isle and was indeed gifted with the gab, which he was willing to demonstrate at all times.

We were all set to go and had started our convoy to the coast when the German High Command decided to call it a day. It is just possible that they heard we were coming but I doubt it. They must have had enough when Hitler opted out in his Berlin bunker.

The VE celebrations stopped us in our tracks and it took us about two days to get to the landing ship tank which was to take us over to Belgium, then about another two days to reach a jubilant HQ which was still celebrating. When we got our marching orders, my heart sank, and I wondered if it had all been in vain – our posting turned out to be Hamburg, in the north-west of Germany – it couldn't have been further away from where I wanted to be. My mind went back over the unbelievable training course – riding through the woods with the motorbike, then up and down old shale bings, through the water and the mud of the tank testing grounds, until I thought I would never be able to walk normally again.

On top of this there was the gruelling physical side: everything had to be done in a set time, followed by intensive map reading and orienteering day-and-night schemes. This was interspersed with square-bashing under a guard drill sergeant instructor and weapon training ranging from the revolver to the bazooka. After all that, I had ended up in Hamburg. It was the old story of Fate kidding you along and then kicking you in the teeth. Then again, the options had been quite clear. A return to the Signals at Catterick, a posting to Scottish Command, or the one I had been offered at Intelligence Corps. Even now I have to admit that this was still the one that would be my first choice, although it was definitely in the wrong direction.

HQ sent us on our way with a sharp reminder to pay close attention to our map reading. Just before the capitulation one of our sections had gone off and when they arrived at their destination they found themselves in a town still occupied by the German army.

The 500-mile run up to the north-east was a real slog. All sorts of convoys were on the move, including heavy and light armour, troops and provisions. Our bikes were red-hot trying to keep our little lot together and eventually we reached the outskirts of Hamburg. Then the picture of the devastation caused by our Air Force began to unfold.

You could see it and you could smell it, but you couldn't comprehend it. It was like a canvas painted by some manic depressive artist who had lost control of his theme and ended up painting a lot of rubbish without being able to stop and carried on and on painting this nightmarish landscape. When we crossed the Elbe bridge into Hamburg the nightmare continued for mile after mile and the smell got worse. Hundreds of thousands of women and children and old people had either been blown to pieces or burned to death in this area. Before the war the residents here had regarded the British as their cousins because of their close relationship in the shipping business. They found it incomprehensible that we could even think of bombing them, but unfortunately, geographically, they were about the nearest German target that was worth bombing.

I still hadn't got used to all the empty shells of buildings as we passed through the main square where the Rathaus was situated and carried on northwards until we reached the dome of the Hauptbahnhof and then turned into the first street after this on the left. We stopped at a small hotel which was to be our home until we were demobbed. There were two fairly similar hotels adjacent to ours, and all three were occupied by security sections. The staff in these establishments had been retained, including cooks, cleaners and chambermaids, so we would eat, sleep and drink here in comparative comfort.

42

Early next morning after breakfast, we went down town to the Priengebaude on the corner of the Alster, a little lake in the centre of Hamburg, and occupied our new offices on the top of the building. Here we would do all our interrogations and paper work.

Our next trip was down to the dock area in St Pauli and to our dock offices on the Landungsbrugge. From here we would operate with our fleet of launches and cover the arrival and departure of all shipping on the river. This was one of the world's main ports. Our job included checking crews and passengers, and issuing shore-leave passes where authorised. With all this in mind, it wasn't surprising that our good captain was soon promoted to the rank of major, which suited him and us much better, and with it went the nice Mercedes he had acquired from somewhere. Paddy loved the Merc too.

It took time to get used to the black market that operated in the street outside our hotel. Our trucks and motorbikes parked outside made no difference to the people who traded there. We had to take it in our stride, and in one instance it was quite handy. When I was asked to do a report on the black market, I would go out and arrest someone, bring them in and get the information that I wanted, then give them a drink and turn them loose. I would carry on like this until I had all the information that I needed.

Meantime people were taking rubble out of the houses and carrying bricks and wood back in; glass was being replaced in the windows. It was like watching a colony of ants. Very quickly things were beginning to take some sort of shape and order. I noticed from my bedroom window that two girls occupied a bedroom on the ground floor of the house opposite. One was a very pretty blonde and the other a not-so-pretty brunette, presumably sisters. They certainly showed a healthy interest in what was going on in our rooms, and I made a note to look into the situation when we were a bit more settled. In the first month we were in Hamburg we were tied down with interrogations and arrestable categories till we couldn't think clearly. What really amazed me was the number of people who wanted to denounce someone. It quickly became apparent that the majority of these cases were attempts to settle grudges, and most of them were time-wasters we could do without.

The major called Bob and me into his office one morning to ask if we would do one of the town sections a favour. They had been trying to arrest one of the shipping magnates for some time, but with no success. Our boss had been having a drink with this section officer and asked if maybe a couple of his boys could have a go at picking up the magnate, to which the section officer readily agreed, probably thinking we would have no more success than them. When we were told it was Herr Essberger, I was really surprised, as his shipping line was extremely well known and he would most certainly be very well protected from unwelcome callers. His office building was on the other side of the Alster lake, almost opposite our town office. We were told that his personal office was on the first floor, and on the days he didn't stay in the office, he almost invariably made it a morning visit. The other section's surveillance team claimed that he was never seen entering or leaving the building, so he had to have another way in. Bob and I opted for the direct approach and hoped for the best.

The next morning, at about ten-thirty, we pulled up in front of the building next to Herr Essberger's. Bob parked the truck and I slung over my shoulder the sten-gun that I had decided to bring along for effect. True to form, Bob tucked in the holster cover of his .38 so that the gun butt stuck out. This, along with his black beret, made him look very intimidating. Then we walked along to the Essberger front door.

When we reached the front steps, the action became fast and decisive. We were through the front door like a couple of greyhounds at White City, and I passed through the receptionist's office before she could blink or press any buttons. I pulled the plug on the switchboard. Our next move was to usher the confused young lady out of her office and lock the door, putting the key in my pocket. The three of us then entered the lift and went up to the first floor where there was no mistaking the door that led to the boss's office. We signalled the girl to be quiet and knocked gently on the door. A polite voiced asked us to enter.

I didn't know what to expect but I certainly was surprised at the reception we received. The nice-looking gentleman behind the large desk looked only momentarily surprised at the sight of such unlikely visitors, but breeding tells, and with a charming smile he asked us in beautiful English how he could help us. I explained to him that we were from Intelligence and that he was now under arrest because of his rank in the Party. Personally, I thought he looked quite relieved, as though he was glad it was finally over. We got him to empty the contents of his safe and all the papers on his desk into a couple of boxes and, after returning the key of the office to the young lady, we left quietly. We returned to our office and handed over the boxes and

Herr Essberger to our very surprised major, who thanked us and gave us an approving nod.

43

The Germans were working like beavers in the rubble of the city, clearing roads, tidying up and digging out the remains of their shattered homes, slowly making places to live in. Brickies, joiners and plumbers were working all the hours God sent to make the ruined buildings habitable again. Money was useless, although almost anything could be procured on the black market. The shops were empty and only the strictest supply of rations could be bought on coupons and, as non-fraternisation was in vogue, help from the troops was not yet a possibility. This is where we were a thorn in the side of the Military Police. We carried a card that authorised us to carry civilians in our vehicles and to consort with them in the line of duty. We often had to produce this and leave a very disgruntled MP behind, especially when our passenger happened to be a pretty girl. Something else that got up their noses was our permits to carry automatics instead of the regulation .38s. We were even issued with Mauser semi-automatics in their strange wooden holsters, which could be clipped on the butt, although the only time I ever used this weapon was for hunting in the forest outside the city.

We eventually conquered the huge pile of routine interrogations which, in turn, led us on to the more interesting work of individual investigations. This required a list of contacts and informants who had to be carefully vetted, so that as little time as possible would be wasted. I had a great stroke of luck when Eric da Silva, one of our section sergeants, asked me if I would take one of his contacts off his hands as he just could not get on with the guy. In all fairness to the German, Eric felt that he had a lot to offer. This led me into a friendship which lasted for many years and was very productive.

Jack Rothschenk was born a Hamburger. He was a little smaller than myself, stockily built, and he spoke fluent English with a broad Brooklyn accent, which he had acquired in the States. He was a broken-down German version of Edward G. Robinson with the voice to match and, to crown it all, he was a seamen's union boss. This was, of course, ideal for the type of information we were looking for and paid off handsomely in the long run. His mode of transport was an old American Studebaker and it suited him and his extravert personality perfectly. Jack was happily married to both his wife and his secretary, who was completely indispensable to him and lived in his office most of the time, though her home was in a little town called Gluckstadt ('Happy Town'), situated near the mouth of the River Elbe.

Benny and I made a racing visit to Gluckstadt one day after a phone call from Jack informed us that Deputy Führer Martin Bormann would be smuggled out in a freighter from there. After our enquiries were complete, we realised that we were a little too late, which was a great pity as it would have put us into the history books. One of our sections did pick up Von Ribbentrop, who had been the German Foreign Minister, so presumably he was in Hamburg trying to find a way out. This was, of course, why we had so many sections and such a strong presence in the port.

Lunchbreak was my favourite time of the day. We would head for the Sergeants' Mess, which was in the

Ratsweinkeller in the basement of the Town Hall. The town councillors certainly knew how to live off the ratepayers, as the restaurant and bars below the town hall were opulent. Here we would dine and drink in a manner that had no resemblence to the world outside. These were definitely the best two hours of the day, and set me up for the rigours of the afternoon's work.

Most of the evenings turned out to be serious drinking sessions, though this slowly changed as we began to sort out some kind of love life, which after all was inevitable. I still thought about Traudl but couldn't come up with a solution. I didn't dare risk writing in case the letter was intercepted, which would have led to her arrest and possible death. I decided that patience was required for a while longer. My hormones were not listening again, which was not surprising considering the amount of talent parading around us advertising its availability.

I had craftily solved the problem of how to get at the promiscuous young blonde across the road, who kept giving me the green light from her bedroom window at the front of the house. The section trucks were parked on the other side of the road, so I asked Benny if he would reverse his vehicle up on to the pavement so that the rear end would be right outside blondie's bedroom window, with just enough space for me to climb into the truck. The next step was to tell the young lady of this strategy and arrange a time for our first meeting. This worked out nicely and the meeting duly took place with me sitting on her window sill and her kneeling on a chair inside her bedroom.

Things progressed from then on and Ingeborg and I had a lot of fun together. I was amazed at how little knowledge I had about sex and how to enjoy it, but a spell in Hamburg was a revelation. The Reeperbahn is world-renowned, but I recommend a guided tour with someone well-connected with the area, otherwise it could turn out to be most alarming, and has been known to be fatal.

Jack Rothschenk knew the Reeperbahn and the St Pauli area intimately and was well liked and accepted by the Red Light fraternity. Naturally, I got to know a lot of people in this area as it was adjacent to the Landungsbrucke where our dock offices were. It took me some time to notice that Jack never paid for anything when we were having a night out in St Pauli; there was so much of the old boy network in operation that I was quite amazed. We could go to places where they served T-bone steaks and eggs, and yet some people had difficulty in obtaining the rations shown on their books. Hard liquor was almost unobtainable, but this is where I was a godsend, as our rations were quite generous and of very high quality. We received invitations from people who wouldn't normally have given us the time of day.

One such person was a friend of Jack's called Cesar. He was the oldest son of a patrician Hamburg family with a huge business interest in the dock area. Cesar was a graduate of Oxford, which became apparent when he spoke English; under normal circumstances he wouldn't have consorted with the likes of Jack or myself but, as they say, war makes strange bedfellows. One of his main weaknesses was alcohol, and why shouldn't he befriend a good provider of the hard stuff when it was in extremely short supply? He was great company, and the three of us had some memorable parties, some in very high-class company.

This worked out wonderfully well for me, as Americans in Stuttgart had asked for co-operation from Hamburg on some underground activities which affected them. The boss asked me if there was any possibility of getting close to the source. I talked to Jack about it and he said that the old Anti-Nazi Committee might be able to help. They had a meeting arranged for a couple of weeks later and, as Jack was a member, he would be there; I asked him if it would be possible for me to be present. His answer was an emphatic 'No', as the mere sight of a uniform anywhere near the meeting place would cause an automatic cancellation. I then asked him if I would be admitted with him if I was in civvy clothes and he agreed that this would be allowed. Intelligence Corps personnel were allowed to wear civvy clothes in the UK but not abroad, so I had a problem. There was no point in asking the boss because he was duty-bound to say 'No', but what he didn't know wouldn't do him any harm. So, Jack and I visited the Merchant Navy tailor and he made me a double-breasted dark suit. The reason I wanted to be at the meeting in person was that I wanted to hear Jack ask the right questions and to hear the answers personally.

We duly attended the meeting and got what sounded like the information we were looking for, though only further investigation would show if this was of any consequence. By a horrible coincidence it led us into the middle of the social group we had been partying with. We had been seeing quite a lot of one charming couple who lived in a big flat in town. It was fairly obvious that Cesar was in love with the wife, whose name was Jacquie, though he was always circumspect when husband Heinz was about. Jack and I were shocked when we were told that the key figure in the equation was indeed our friend Heinz. I passed the information on to the boss, and when he asked me to give him a detailed report, I told him that I could give him an abridged version. Immediately he asked if I had been naughty and broken some rules, and when I admitted that this was indeed the case, he smiled his most charming smile and told me to make it as plausible as possible.

One month later Heinz was dead. He was apparently killed in a freak accident where his head was crushed between his car and a caravan he was using. The funeral was very private.

44

This type of hard work and hard drinking went on until I was finally demobbed in January 1946. After collecting my civvy clothes at Redford Barracks in Edinburgh, I went home to Mum to enjoy about five months' accumulated leave. All the know-alls said that after about a month of inactivity I would be raring to go back to work, but this didn't happen. First, I arranged to get a passport. This didn't take too long, and while I was waiting for it to come through, I applied for an entry visa to Czechoslovakia, but the authorities said this wouldn't be forthcoming for a long time. Coincidentally, the passport arrived at the same time as a letter from the Control Commission for Germany (CCG) asking if I was interested in returning to Germany in the post of a British Passport Officer.

This new and unexpected development required a lot of thought; I was still a Civil Servant and would be required to return to my parent department. The old me would naturally have done exactly what was expected of me but the new me had no qualms about answering the letter and saying that I would indeed be interested in the proposition, thinking that probably nothing would come of it. I decided to say nothing about the offer to the Engineering Department; I still had a few months' leave left, so it wasn't really relevant.

The first surprise came a few weeks later when I was invited to attend an interview in London. When I saw the competition in the waiting room, I gave up any hopes of a post. There were Group Captains, Lt. Colonels, Naval Officers and Uncle Tom Cobley and all – all out to carry on from where they had left off in the war but, please, not back to civvy street. The only laugh I had was when the security man in the entry hall checked my name against his list and said I would be the gentleman from MI, which flummoxed me until I worked it out – he had me down as Military Intelligence.

The board were very nice and very impressive and I would have given all of them a job. After the interview I was thanked politely and ushered out. I thought that would be the end of it, but a few weeks later another letter arrived from this distinguished panel inviting me for a further inquisition. This time I knew who I was before the doorman told me. In the office, to my surprise, there was an old friend working as chief clerk. He had been one of our section sergeants in Hamburg. Taffy, as he was known to us, told me in confidence that I had finished high in the ratings of the last interview and I was definitely on the short-list for one of the posts. When I asked him why he wasn't on it, he said that he had tried and this was the best that he could do.

The board went over much the same ground as the last time, but with a little more emphasis here and there. Again I was thanked but this time they said I would probably hear from them. Sure enough, a couple of weeks later the final demand arrived, but now there was one discordant note from a member of the panel, who apparently was a senior Civil Servant. He very properly pointed out that I was not in a position to accept the post as I was duty-bound to return to my parent department when my leave was finished – so what did I have in mind? My reply was that if the post was offered to me and the Civil Service didn't release me, then I would offer my resignation and take their job, since I considered it important enough to warrant such action.

There was a flurry of whispers and the result was that I would be allowed to take the job, if I agreed to return to the department when the post became redundant. I was advised to apply for a passport immediately, and there were a few knowing smiles when I said that I already held a current passport. How wrong they were in their thinking.

Details of salary, uniform and rank were worked out, and I was to start as a Control Officer, Grade 3, which was the equivalent rank of captain. I then notified my department of what was happening and reported to my new HQ in Germany, where I was informed that I should have taken over Major Haigh's command in Hamburg, but would I please go to Cuxhaven instead and set up the controls for the arrival of the British Forces married families.

45

After we had escaped, I had asked for promotion and responsibility and it was given to me. The post of BPO was certainly a full-time job, requiring lots of memory work on policy and regulations, with no set hours, but with the usual complete freedom to commandeer staff and accommodation. In Cuxhaven I took over the Yacht Club as our Passport Office and employed the best civilian staff available, though my main help came from the Frontier Control Service personnel.

When the Cuxhaven Control was running smoothly, I was transferred to Hamburg and, after changing the three officers who had been employed there for three new ones who could be trained properly, I settled into Major Haigh's old position with a feeling of justifiable pride. To crown it all I was also promoted to the grade of Control Officer 2, equivalent to the rank of major. So, as far as I was concerned, the wheel had come full circle. It was shortly after this that a letter from Traudl got redirected to me with the good news that she was well – and the bad news that she had got tired of waiting to hear from me and had married a Czech army officer!

46

A rest period was long overdue, and it finally came in the form of a posting to Lübeck, a town which straddles the River Trave, which in turn runs into the Baltic Sea. This reminded me of our POW posting to Bad Karlsbrunn in Sudetenland, as it was a real holiday area and the workload was almost non-existent. I still kept in touch with Hamburg, and it was on one of these trips that fate decided that for me the war was over.

Normally, my driver Hans would have been at the wheel of the Mercedes on our way back from Hamburg, but on this particular beautiful spring day I had decided to drive myself, or perhaps the gods who control these things had decided for us. In any case we passed a young lady smiling by the roadside, with her thumb in the classic hitchhiking position. It has never been my policy to give people lifts but, to my great surprise, my foot went onto the brake pedal and we came to a stop.

When the beautiful face with the lovely tan asked for a lift into Lübeck, who could have refused? By the time we had reached town I had asked her to have dinner with me, but she accepted only after a lot of persuasion. Her name was Franziska, or Frankie for short, and you know the song about Frankie and Johnnie being lovers. Eventually we were, and still are to this day. We were together from then on and in November 1949 we decided to come home and get married.

Knowing Frankie brought me a great inner peace and a stability that had been sadly lacking. Various people remarked on the more estimable character that I became after meeting her. I was offered another promotion but we both decided that enough was enough, and when you think about it, ten years out of your life is surely all that can be expected from you.

So we kissed Germany goodbye and came home.